The Perfect Pajama

The Perfect Pajama

Sleep tight every night with these 21 fun and cute designs

Kristina Nilsson and Jennifer Pirtle

CICO BOOKS

LONDON NEW YORK

Published in 2009 by CICO Books
An imprint of Ryland Peters & Small Ltd

20–21 Jockey's Fields   519 Broadway, 5th Floor
London WC1R 4BW   New York, NY 10012

www.cicobooks.com

10 9 8 7 6 5 4 3 2 1

A CIP catalog record for this book is available from the
Library of Congress and the British Library.

US ISBN-13: 978 1 906525 96 5
UK ISBN-13: 978 1 906525 76 7

Printed in China

Editor: Sarah Hoggett
Design: Christine Wood
Photography: Terry Benson
Illustration: Stephen Dew and Trina Dalziel
Blue Lagoon project design: Rob Merrett
Stylist: Jo Latham

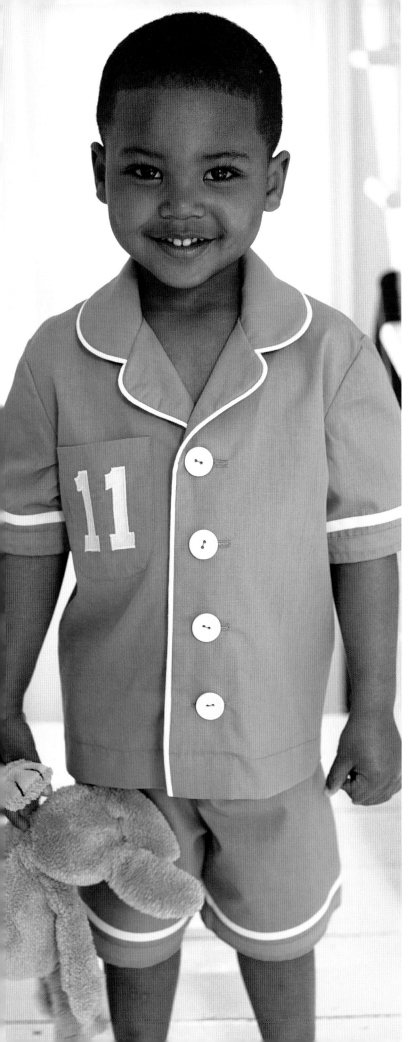

Contents

Introduction

Why should you look any less stylish at bedtime than you do during the day? Armed with this book and a sewing machine, you can create wonderful, personalized pajamas and accessories that are a lot more inspiring than what most shops have to offer. By choosing your own fabrics, adding special trims and details, and sewing the projects yourself, you'll have truly unique nightwear—plus plenty of creative fun along the way!

The Perfect Pajama features three easy-to-use sections, one each for children's pajamas, adults' pajamas, and nighttime accessories. There are 21 gorgeous projects in total, plus comprehensive materials lists and step-by-step instructions. At the back of the book, you'll find a helpful techniques section to carefully guide you through any seemingly tricky steps. The material quantities listed for each project are generous enough for the largest pattern size, so you may want to adjust them according to what size you are making—but keep in mind it is always useful to have extra fabric just in case. Happy sewing and sleep tight!

chapter 1

Good night,
sweetheart

Dolly Mixture

An appliquéd rag doll motif makes this brushed cotton nightshirt extra special. Pink and pretty, with blanket-stitched edges and strawberry buttons, it promises every little girl a good night's sleep!

Cutting and marking

Trace the required pattern pieces onto tissue paper (see page 90) and cut out. Pin the paper pattern pieces to your chosen fabric and cut out, remembering to transfer all reference marks to the fabric pieces (see page 90). Re-using the paper patterns, cut out the required pieces of interfacing and apply them to the wrong side of their fabric counterparts.

Nightshirt

1 Following the manufacturer's instructions, iron fusible bonding web to the back of the felt and gingham fabrics. Using the rag doll template (page 95), draw the doll body and dress pieces on the bonding web backing paper and cut out. Place the rag doll on the right front body piece and iron to fuse the fabrics together.

You will need

2 yd (180 cm) brushed cotton fabric, 56 in. (144 cm) wide

Small piece of skin-colored felt for rag doll body

Small piece of gingham fabric for rag doll dress

90 cm (36 in.) lightweight iron-on interfacing, 36 in. (90 cm) wide

4 in. (10 cm) fusible bonding web, 17 in. (43 cm) wide

5 x ½-in. (20-mm) buttons

Sewing thread to match felt

Hot pink sewing thread

Hot pink embroidery floss (thread)

Brown tapestry yarn for the hair

Sewing machine

Needle and matching sewing threads

Fabric pattern pieces required

Brushed cotton fabric: Left and right front panels, left and right front panel facings, back panel, back neck facing, left and right sleeves, 2 collars, 2 patch pockets

Interfacing: Left and right front panel facings, back neck facing, 2 collars

Take ½-in. (1.5-cm) seam allowances throughout unless otherwise stated.

2 Using matching thread and a very short, narrow zigzag stitch, machine stitch around the edges of each felt piece to cover the raw edges. Change to hot pink thread and stitch around the edges of the doll's gingham dress in the same way.

3 Fold the top edges of the pockets over to the wrong side by 1 in. (3 cm). Press, pin, and machine stitch in place. Using a card template, press under the raw edges of the pocket (see page 92). Place the first pocket on the right front body piece, covering the bottom of the rag doll's dress. Pin in place. Using matching thread, topstitch around the side and bottom edges, stitching as close to the edge as possible. Apply the second pocket to the left front body piece in the same way.

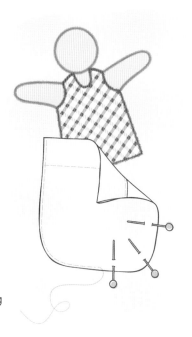

4 With right sides together, machine stitch the front panels to the back panel at the shoulders. Overlock or zigzag stitch the raw edges together, and press the seam allowances toward the front. Make the collar and attach the facings (see page 92).

5 With right sides together, matching the balance marks, pin the right sleeve to the right armhole (see page 93). Stitch the seam, overlock or zigzag stitch the raw edges together, and press toward the sleeve. Repeat for the left sleeve. Match up the underarm and side seam edges and pin in place. Stitch from cuff to hem, overlock or zigzag stitch the edges together, and press the seam allowances toward the front.

6 To finish the cuffs, fold the raw edges over to the wrong side by ⅜ in. (1 cm) and then by another ¾ in. (2 cm), and press. Pin in place, then machine stitch.

7 Overlock or zigzag stitch the raw edge at the hem. With the facing and shirt right sides together, machine stitch along the hem on the facing, taking a 1⅛-in. (3-cm) seam allowance. Turn right side out and push the corners out. Fold the raw edge of the facing over by 1⅛ in. (3 cm), press, pin, and stitch in place.

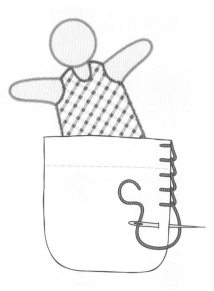

8 Using hot pink embroidery floss (thread), blanket stitch along the whole front edge, hem, and cuffs of the nightshirt, and around the side and bottom edges of the pockets (see page 91).

9 Mark the position of the buttonholes along the right center front and stitch (see page 94), using hot pink thread. Sew buttons to the left center front to correspond.

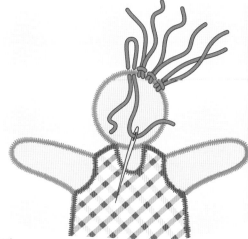

10 Cut 15–20 6-in. (15-cm) strands of brown tapestry yarn for the hair. Thread a needle with a piece of tapestry yarn. Starting at the top of the doll's head, insert the needle just inside the zigzag stitching and bring it back out just outside. Insert the needle again right next to the previous stitch, and bring it back out just inside the zigzag stitching without pulling the thread all the way through, leaving a loop. Unthread the needle, grab both yarn ends and pull them through the loop. Continue applying hair until the top of the doll's head is covered.

11 Hand stitch two little blue dots onto the
doll's face for the eyes. Embroider a pink
mouth using backstitch (see page 91).

Butterflies

These lovely pajamas will brighten up any little girl's bedtime. The gorgeous butterfly border print is trimmed to the max with girly delights. Pink pompoms, super-cute butterfly buttons, pretty rickrack, polka dots—these summery PJs have it all!

Cutting and marking

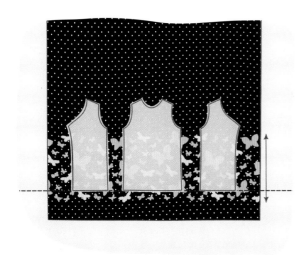

Trace the required pattern pieces onto tissue paper (see page 90) and cut out. Pin the paper pattern pieces to your chosen fabric and cut out, remembering to transfer all reference marks to the fabric pieces (see page 90). When cutting a border print fabric, make sure that the hem edges of the front and back body pieces are level. Re-using the paper patterns, cut out the required pieces of interfacing and apply them to the wrong side of their fabric counterparts.

Shirt

1   With right sides together, stitch the front panels to the back panel at the shoulders. Overlock or zigzag stitch the edges together and press the seam allowances toward the front. Make the collar and attach the facings (see page 92).

2   With right sides together, matching the balance marks, pin the right sleeve to the right armhole (see page 93). Stitch the seam, overlock or zigzag stitch the raw edges together, and press toward the sleeve. Repeat for the left sleeve. Match up the underarm and side seam edges and pin in place. Stitch from cuff to hem, overlock or zigzag stitch the edges together, and press the seams toward the front.

You will need

2¼ yd (2 m) border print fabric, 56 in. (144 cm) wide

28 in. (70 cm) lightweight iron-on interfacing, 36 in. (90 cm) wide

2¾ yd (2.5 m) pink pompom trim

1 yd (100 cm) pink rickrack braid

1¼ yd (1.5 m) elastic, 1 in. (2.5 cm) wide

5 x ¾-in. (18-mm) butterfly-shaped buttons

Sewing machine

Needle and matching sewing threads

Fabric pattern pieces required

Shirt
Border print fabric: Left and right front panels, left and right front panel facings, back panel, back neck facing, left and right sleeves

Interfacing: Left and right front panel facings, back neck facing, 2 collars

Shorts
Border print fabric: Left front and back legs, right front and back legs

Take ½-in. (1.5-cm) seam allowances throughout unless otherwise stated.

3

Fold the raw edges of the cuffs over to the wrong side by ⅜ in.(1 cm) and then by ¾ in. (2 cm), and press. Pin in place and machine stitch. Measure the cuff circumference on the garment and cut two pieces of pompom trim to that measurement. Pin the trim on the sleeves and stitch along the tape to attach, using a half-presser foot so that you can stitch close to the pompoms.

4 Overlock or zigzag stitch the raw edge at the hem. With the facing and shirt right sides together, stitch along the hem on the facing, taking a 1⅛-in. (3-cm) seam allowance. Turn right side out and push the corners out. Fold the remaining hem edge over by 1⅛ in. (3 cm), press, pin, and stitch in place. Measure the circumference of the hem and cut a piece of pompom trim to that measurement. Pin the trim around the hem and stitch along the tape to attach, using a half-presser foot.

5

Starting just below the top button position, place rickrack braid on the front facing, lining it up with the facing edge. Pin it in place, going up around the collar and back down toward the center front, finishing just below the top button position on the other side. Stitch down the center of the rickrack to attach.

6 Mark the position of the buttonholes along the right center front and stitch (see page 94). Sew buttons along the left center front to correspond.

Shorts

1. Overlock or zigzag stitch the raw side edges of the legs and crotch, leaving the top edges and hems unfinished. Assemble the shorts (see page 93), pressing all seams open as you go.

2. At the waist, fold the edge over to the wrong side by ⅜ in. (1 cm) and then again by 1⅛ in. (3 cm). Press, pin, and machine stitch in place, stopping 1½ in. (4 cm) away from the top edge at the center back. Attach a safety pin to one end of the elastic and thread it through waist channel. Remove the safety pin. Hand stitch the ends of the elastic together. Hand stitch the gap at the center back closed.

3. At the hems, fold the edge over to the wrong side by ⅜ in. (1 cm) and then by ¾ in. (2 cm). Press, pin in place, and machine stitch. Measure the hem circumference and cut two pieces of pompom trim to that measurement. Pin the trim on the legs and stitch along the tape to attach, using a half-presser foot.

Sail Away

Any little boy or girl wearing this lovely nightshirt is sure to dream of lazy summer days by the seaside! Staying true to the nautical theme, these PJs feature beautiful blues with splashes of red, white, and yellow.

Cutting and marking

Trace the required pattern pieces onto tissue paper (see page 90) and cut out. Pin the paper pattern pieces to your chosen fabric and cut out, remembering to transfer all reference marks to the fabric pieces (see page 90). Re-using the paper patterns, cut out the required pieces of interfacing and apply them to the wrong side of their fabric counterparts.

Nightshirt

1 Fold the top edge of each patch pocket over to the wrong side by 1 in. (3 cm). Press, pin, and machine stitch in place. Using a card template, press under the raw edges of the pockets (see page 92). Pin the pockets to the front of the nightshirt and topstitch around the side and bottom edges, stitching as close to the edges as possible. Change to a yellow contrast thread and zigzag topstitch around the pocket edges. Do not back tack at the start or finish; instead, pull the threads through to the inside of the garment and tie off.

You will need

2 yd (180 cm) light blue fabric, 56 in. (144 cm) wide

12 in. (30 cm) lightweight dark blue fabric, 56 in. (144 cm) wide

Scraps of white, red, and blue-and-white striped fabric for appliqué

36 in. (90 cm) lightweight iron-on interfacing, 36 in. (90 cm) wide

1 yd (1 m) fusible bonding web, 17 in. (43 cm) wide

6 x ¾-in. (18-mm) yellow buttons

Yellow, white, and red contrast sewing threads

Sewing machine

Needle and matching sewing threads

Fabric pattern pieces required

Light blue fabric: Left and right front panels, left and right front panel facings, back panel, back neck facing, left and right sleeves, 2 collars, 2 patch pockets

Interfacing: Left and right front panel facings, back neck facing, 2 collars

Take ½-in. (1.5-cm) seam allowances throughout unless otherwise stated.

2 With right sides together, machine stitch the front panels to the back panel at the shoulders. Overlock or zigzag stitch the edges together, and press toward the front. Make the collar and attach the facings (see page 92).

3 With right sides together, matching the balance marks, pin the right sleeve to the right armhole (see page 93). Stitch the seam, overlock or zigzag stitch the raw edges together, and press toward the sleeve. Repeat for the left sleeve.

4 Match up the underarm and side seam edges and pin in place. Machine stitch from cuff to hem, overlock or zigzag stitch the raw edges together, and press the seams toward the front.

5

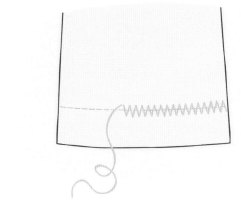

To finish the cuffs, fold the raw edges over to the wrong side by ⅜ in. (1 cm) and then by ¾ in. (2 cm) and press. Pin and machine stitch in place. Change to a contrast yellow thread and zigzag topstitch along the cuff hem line, covering the existing stitching.

6

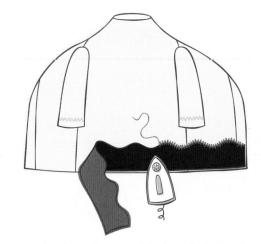

Measure the circumference of the hem, including the facings. Cut a piece of dark blue fabric to this length, 8 in. (20 cm) deep. Following the manufacturer's instructions, iron fusible bonding web to the back of the dark blue fabric. Draw a wave design along the top edge of the backing paper and cut it out. Aligning the raw edges, position the wave trim along the hem edge and iron to fuse the fabrics together. Using a short, narrow zigzag stitch and matching thread, machine stitch around the edges of the hem trim to cover the raw edges.

7

Following the manufacturer's instructions, iron fusible bonding web onto the back of white, red, and blue-and-white striped fabric pieces. Using the sailing boat template on page 95, draw the required shapes on the backing paper and cut out. Place the sailing boat on the front body, partly covering the wave hem appliqué. Iron to fuse the fabrics together. Using white thread, machine stitch around the boat and sails to cover the raw edges, and stitch a white mast between the boat and sails. Change to red thread for the flag, and also stitch a red stripe across the boat.

8 With the facing and shirt right sides together, stitch along the hem on the facing, taking a 1⅛-in. (3-cm) seam allowance. Turn right side out and push the corners out. Fold the hem edge over to the wrong side by 1⅛ in. (3 cm), press, pin, and machine stitch in place. Using a yellow contrast thread, run a zigzag topstitching line all along the front edges.

9 Mark the position of the buttonholes along one side of the center front and stitch (see page 94). Sew the buttons along the other side of the center front to correspond.

Stars and Stripes

Mixing and matching different prints is a great, easy way of updating classic pajamas. This combination of horizontal and vertical stripes, together with a fun star print, creates a playful look. Add some zing by stitching around the appliqué motifs in a contrasting color.

Cutting and marking

Trace the required pattern pieces onto tissue paper (see page 90) and cut out. Pin the paper pattern pieces to your chosen fabric and cut out, remembering to transfer all reference marks to the fabric pieces (see page 90).

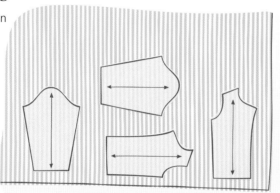

When cutting the fronts and sleeves, cut one side with horizontal stripes and the other with vertical stripes. The back has vertical stripes. Re-using the paper patterns, cut out the required pieces of interfacing and apply them to the wrong side of their fabric counterparts.

Shirt

1 Following the manufacturer's instructions, iron fusible bonding web onto the back of the white fabric. Using the star template on page 95, transfer the star design onto the backing paper and cut it out. Fold the top edge of the patch pocket over to the wrong side by 1 in. (3 cm) and press. Pin in place and topstitch. Peel the backing paper off the bonding web, place the star in the center of the pocket, and iron to fuse the fabrics together. Using a very short, narrow zigzag stitch and red thread for contrast, machine stitch around the star to cover the raw edges.

You will need

1¾ yd (150 cm) striped fabric, 56 in. (144 cm) wide

¾ yd (70 cm) small star fabric, 56 in. (144 cm) wide

1 yd (100 cm) large star fabric, 56 in. (144 cm) wide

6 in. (15 cm) solid (plain) fabric, 56 in. (144 cm) wide

Small piece of white fabric

28 in. (70 cm) lightweight iron-on interfacing, 36 in. (90 cm) wide

60 in. (150 cm) elastic, 1 in. (2.5 cm) wide

4 in. (10 cm) fusible bonding web, 17 in. (44 cm) wide

4 x ⅝-in. (16-mm) buttons

Red sewing thread

Sewing machine

Needle and matching sewing threads

Fabric pattern pieces required

Shirt

Striped fabric: Left and right front panels, back panel, left and right sleeves

Small star fabric: Left and right front panel facings, back neck facing, 2 collars, 2 cuff bands

Solid (plain) fabric: 1 patch pocket

Interfacing: Left and right front panel facings, back neck facing, 2 collars

Pants

Large star fabric: Left front and back legs, right front and back legs

Striped fabric: 2 hem bands

Take ½-in. (1.5-cm) seam allowances throughout unless otherwise stated.

2 Using a card template, press under the side and bottom edges of the pocket (see page 92). Pin the pocket to the right front of the shirt and stitch in place, stitching as close to the edge of pocket as possible.

3 With right sides together, stitch the front panels to the back panel at the shoulders. Overlock or zigzag stitch the edges together and press the seam allowances toward the front. Make the collar and attach the facings (see page 92).

4 With right sides together, matching the balance marks, pin the right sleeve to the right armhole (see page 93). Stitch the seam, overlock or zigzag stitch the raw edges together, and press toward the sleeve. Repeat for the left sleeve. Match up the underarm and side seam edges and pin in place. Stitch from cuff to hem, overlock or zigzag stitch the edges together, and press the seams toward the front.

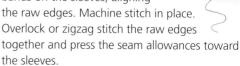

5 With right sides together, stitch the short edges of each cuff band together to make a loop. Press the seams open. With wrong sides together, aligning the raw edges, fold each cuff band in half widthwise and press the edge. Pin the cuff bands on the sleeves, aligning the raw edges. Machine stitch in place. Overlock or zigzag stitch the raw edges together and press the seam allowances toward the sleeves.

6 Overlock or zigzag stitch the raw edge at the hem. With the facings and shirt right sides together, stitch along the hem on the facings, taking a 1⅛-in. (3-cm) seam allowance. Turn right side out and push the corners out. Fold the remaining hem edge over by 1⅛ in. (3 cm), press, pin, and machine stitch in place.

7 Mark the position of the buttonholes along the left center front and stitch (see page 94). Sew buttons along the right center front to correspond.

Pants

1 Overlock or zigzag stitch the raw side edges of the legs and crotch, leaving the top edges and hems unfinished. Assemble the pants (see page 93), pressing all seams open as you go.

2 At the waist, fold the edge over to the wrong side by ⅜ in. (1 cm) and then again by 1⅛ in. (3 cm). Press, pin, and machine stitch in place, stopping 1½ in. (4 cm) away from the top edge at the center back. Attach a safety pin to one end of the elastic and thread it through the waist channel. Remove the safety pin. Hand stitch the ends of the elastic together. Hand stitch the gap at the center back closed.

With right sides together, machine stitch the short edges of each hem band together to make a loop. Press the seams open. With wrong sides together, aligning the raw edges, fold each hem band in half widthwise and press the edge. Pin the hem bands on the legs, aligning the raw edges. Stitch in place. Overlock or zigzag stitch the raw edges together and press the seam allowances toward the hem.

Dream Team

Budding athletes will love these cool pajamas. Made from vibrant turquoise fabric, they're packed full of great details, including fresh white and green trims. This is nightwear fit for the sports hero of the future!

Cutting and marking

Trace the required pattern pieces onto tissue paper (see page 90) and cut out. Pin the paper pattern pieces to your chosen fabric and cut out, remembering to transfer all reference marks to the fabric pieces (see page 90). Re-using the paper patterns, cut out the required pieces of interfacing and apply them to the wrong side of their fabric counterparts.

Shirt

1 Following the manufacturer's instructions, iron fusible bonding web onto the back of the white appliqué fabric. Using the small number 1 template on page 95, draw four numbers on the backing paper and cut them out. Fold the top edge of the patch pocket over to the wrong side by 1 in. (3 cm) and press the edge. Pin in place and topstitch. Place two number ones in the center of the pocket, keeping the other two numbers for the shorts pocket. Iron to fuse the fabrics together.

2 Using a very short, narrow zigzag stitch, machine stitch around the edges of the numbers to cover the raw edges.

You will need

2¼ yd (200 cm) turquoise fabric, 56 in. (144 cm) wide

½ yd (50 cm) white fabric, 56 in. (144 cm) wide

8 in. (20 cm) green fabric, 56 in. (144 cm) wide

28 in. (70 cm) lightweight iron-on interfacing, 36 in. (90 cm) wide

2¼ yd (200 cm) green cotton ribbon, ½ in. (1.5 cm) wide

2¼ yd (200 cm) white cotton ribbon, ¼ in. (7mm) wide

2¼ yd (200 cm) green cord

12 in. (30 cm) fusible bonding web, 17 in. (44 cm) wide

4 x ¾-in. (18-mm) buttons

White and green sewing threads

Sewing machine

Needle and matching sewing threads

Fabric pattern pieces required

Shirt

Turquoise fabric: Left and right front panels, left and right front panel facings, back panel, back neck facing, left and right sleeves, 2 collars, 1 patch pocket

Interfacing: Left and right front panel facings, back neck facing, 2 collars

Shorts

Turquoise fabric: Left front and back legs, right front and back legs, 1 patch pocket

Take ½-in. (1.5-cm) seam allowances throughout unless otherwise stated.

3 Using a card template, press under the side and bottom edges of the pocket (see page 92). Pin the pocket to the right front of shirt and stitch in place, stitching as close to the edge of the pocket as possible.

4 Following the manufacturer's instructions, iron fusible bonding web to the back of the green fabric. Using the outside line of the large number one template on page 95, draw two numbers on the backing paper and cut them out. Place the numbers on the back body piece and iron to fuse the fabrics together. Now use the inside line of the large number one template to make two white number ones. Center them on the green numbers and iron them in place. Use a very short, narrow zigzag stitch and matching threads, machine stitch around the edges of both the green and white numbers to cover the raw edges.

5 With right sides together, stitch the front panels to the back panel at the shoulders. Overlock or zigzag stitch the edges together and press the seam allowances toward the front.

6

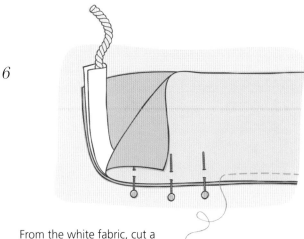

From the white fabric, cut a bias strip measuring 1½ x 48 in. (4 x 120 cm). (Join two pieces together to get the right length if necessary; see page 94.) Place piping cord at the center of the bias strip and fold the edges over, trapping the cord inside. Aligning the raw edges, sandwich the bias strip between the two collar pieces and stitch, using a half-presser foot so that you can stitch close to the piping cord.

7 Attach the facings (see page 92), inserting piping along the front edges in the same way as for the collar, up to the point where the collar joins the facing.

8 With right sides together, matching the balance marks, pin the right sleeve to the right armhole (see page 93). Stitch the seam, overlock or zigzag stitch the raw edges together, and press toward the sleeve. Repeat for the left sleeve. Match up the underarm and side seam edges and pin in place. Stitch from cuff to hem, overlock or zigzag stitch the edges together, and press the seam allowances toward the front.

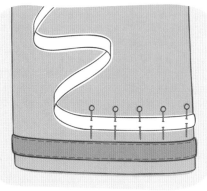

9 Fold the raw edges of the cuffs over to the wrong side by ⅜ in. (1 cm) and then by ¾ in. (2 cm). Press the edge, pin, and stitch in place. Place green cotton ribbon ¼ in. (0.5 cm) away from the cuff edge, covering the stitching line. Pin in place and stitch very close to each edge of the ribbon to attach. Now place white cotton ribbon ¼ in. (0.5 cm) away from the green ribbon edge and attach in the same way.

10 Overlock or zigzag stitch the raw edge at the hem. With the facing and shirt right sides together, stitch along the hem on the facing, taking a 1⅛-in. (3-cm) seam allowance. Turn right side out and push the corners out. Fold the remaining hem edge over by 1⅛ in. (3 cm), press, pin, and stitch in place.

11 Mark the position of the buttonholes along the left center front and stitch (see page 94). Sew buttons along the right center front to correspond.

Shorts

1 Overlock or zigzag stitch the raw side edges of the legs and crotch, leaving the top edges and hems unfinished. Assemble the shorts (see page 93), pressing all seams open as you go.

2 At the waist, fold the edge over to the wrong side by ⅜ in. (1 cm) and then by 1⅛ in. (3 cm). Press to make a crease line. Open the fold out again and mark the buttonhole positions on both sides, ⅜ in. (1 cm) below the crease line and ¾ in. (2 cm) away from the center front. Make the buttonholes (see page 94).

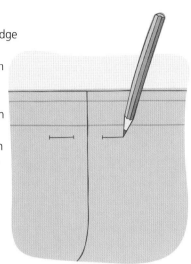

3 Stitch the fold in place. Attach a safety pin to one end of the green cord and thread it through the buttonholes in the waist channel.

4 Fold the raw hem edges over to the wrong side by ⅜ in. (1 cm) and then by ¾ in. (2 cm). Press the edge, pin, and stitch in place. Place green cotton ribbon ¼ in. (0.5 cm) away from the hem edge, covering the stitching line. Pin in place and stitch very close to each edge of the ribbon to attach. Now place white cotton ribbon ¼ in. (0.5 cm) away from the green ribbon edge and attach in the same way.

Cheery Checks

Gingham check fabric is readily available in a variety of different colors. Mix them up to create these sweet boy's pajamas. The simple tunic top is easy to make and comfortable to wear; add some texture with stab stitching around the neckline, cuffs, and pockets.

Cutting and marking

Trace the required pattern pieces onto tissue paper (see page 90) and cut out. Pin the paper pattern pieces to your chosen fabric and cut out, remembering to transfer all reference marks to the fabric pieces (see page 90). Do not cut the neckline keyhole split! Re-using the paper patterns, cut out the required pieces of interfacing and apply them to the wrong side of their fabric counterparts.

Shirt

1 Fold the top edge of each patch pocket over to the wrong side by 1 in. (3 cm) and press the edge. Pin in place and machine stitch. Using a card template, press under the side and bottom edges of the pocket (see page 92). Pin to the front of the shirt and topstitch in place, stitching as close to the edge as possible.

2 With right sides together, stitch the front panels to the back panel at the shoulders. Overlock or zigzag stitch the edges together and press seam allowances toward the front. Now stitch the front facing to the back facing at the shoulders. Press seam allowances toward the front. Overlock or zigzag stitch the outside facing edge.

3 Using tailor's chalk, mark out the keyhole slit line on the front facing. Place the facing on the body, matching up the shoulder seams and aligning the raw edges. Pin in place along the neckline and keyhole slit line.

You will need

2¼ yd (200 cm) red gingham fabric, 56 in. (144 cm) wide

12 in. (30 cm) blue gingham fabric, 56 in. (144 cm) wide

28 in. (70 cm) lightweight iron-on interfacing, 36 in. (90 cm) wide

Red and blue embroidery flosses (threads)

Sewing machine

Needle and matching sewing threads

Fabric pattern pieces required

Shirt

Red gingham: Front panel (place on fold of fabric to cut 1 piece), front facing, back panel, back neck facing, left and right sleeves

Blue gingham: 2 patch pockets, 2 cuff bands

Interfacing: Front panel, back neck panel

Pants

Red gingham: Left front and back legs, right front and back legs

Blue gingham: 2 patch pockets, 2 hem bands

Take ½-in. (1.5-cm) seam allowances throughout unless otherwise stated.

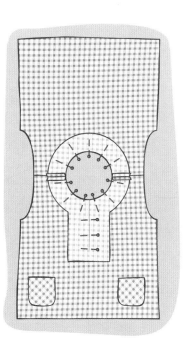

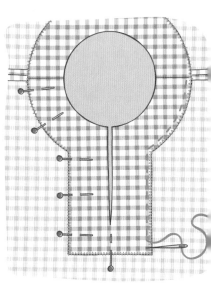

4 Starting at the center back, stitch along the neckline. Stop with the needle down ¼ in. (0.5 cm) away from the keyhole slit line. Turn the work around and stitch along the slit line. About 1 in. (3 cm) before the end of the slit line, reduce the stitch length to reinforce the seam. At the end of the slit, narrow the seam allowance to nothing. Stop with the needle down, turn the work around, and stitch up toward the top neck on the other side of the slit line.

5 Cut down the slit line, stopping just before the point. Trim the seam allowances along the neckline to ¼ in. (0.5 cm). Turn the facing to the inside of the shirt and press the neckline edge.

6 With right sides together, matching the balance marks, pin the right sleeve to the right armhole (see page 93), Stitch the seam, overlock or zigzag stitch the raw edges together, and press toward the sleeve. Repeat for the left sleeve. Match up the underarm and side seam edges and pin in place. Stitch from cuff to hem, overlock or zigzag stitch the edges together, and press toward the front.

7 With right sides together, machine stitch the short edges of each cuff band together to make a loop. Press the seams open. With wrong sides together, aligning the raw edges, fold each cuff band in half widthwise and press the edge. Place the cuff bands on the sleeves, aligning the raw edges. Pin and machine stitch in place. Overlock or zigzag stitch the raw edges together and press the seam allowance toward the hem.

8 Turn the raw edge of the hem under by ⅜ in. (1 cm) and then by 1⅛ in. (3 cm). Press, pin in place, and stitch.

9 On the inside of the shirt, pin the facing to the body to hold it in place. Using blue embroidery floss, stab stitch along the facing edge (see page 91), making small, even stitches that are the same size on both sides of the fabric. Using red embroidery floss, stab stitch along the pocket edges and cuff bands.

Pants

1 Fold the top edge of each pocket over to the wrong side by 1 in. (3 cm). Press, pin in place, and machine stitch. Using a card template, press the raw side and bottom edges of the pocket under (see page 92). Pin the pockets to the left and right front legs and topstitch in place, stitching as close to the pocket edges as possible.

2 Overlock or zigzag stitch the raw side edges of the legs and crotch, leaving the top edges and hems unfinished. Assemble the pants (see page 93), pressing all seams open as you go.

3 With right sides together, machine stitch the short edges of each hem band together to make a loop. Press the seams open. With wrong sides together, aligning the raw edges, fold each hem band in half widthwise and press the edge. Place the hem bands on the legs, aligning the raw edges. Pin and machine stitch in place. Overlock or zigzag stitch the raw edges together and press the seam allowances toward the hem.

4 At the waist, fold the edge over to the wrong side by ⅜ in. (1 cm) and then by 1⅛ in. (3 cm). Press the edge to make a crease line. Open the fold out again and mark the buttonhole positions on both sides, ½ in. (1.5 cm) down from the crease line and ¾ in. (2 cm) away from the center front. Make the buttonholes (see page 94).

5

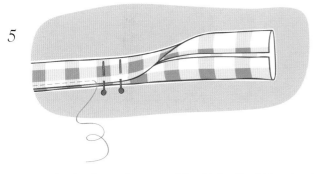

To make the drawstring, cut a 2¾ x 39-in. (7 x 100-cm) strip of blue gingham. Fold the strip in half lengthwise and press the edge to make a crease line. Open the fold out again, then fold each edge in to meet the center crease line. Fold the strip in half again, pin the edge, and machine stitch along the edge.

6 Attach a safety pin to one end of the drawstring and thread it through the waist channel buttonholes.

7 Using red embroidery floss, stab stitch along the pocket edges and hem bands.

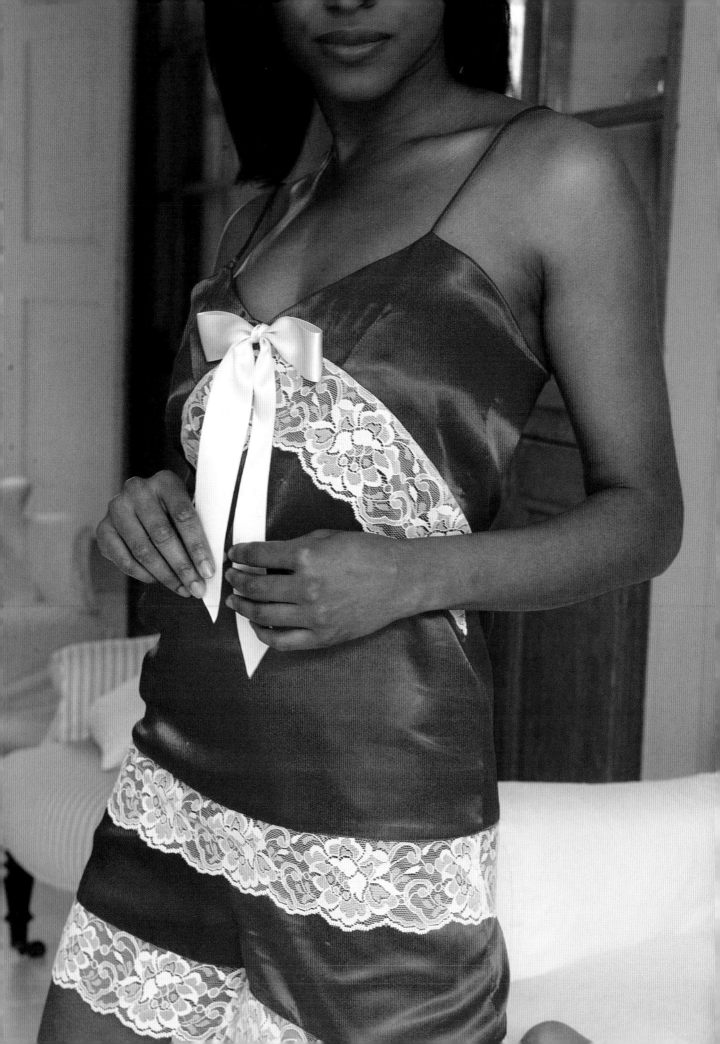

chapter 2

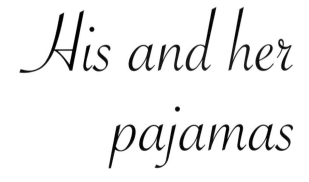

His and her pajamas

Rock 'n' Roll

These cute 1950s-inspired pajamas are packed full of fun details. There is zingy red topstitching and buttonholes, a lovely pleat detail on the sleeves and legs, and a pocket with personalized name emblem. The pink polka-dot fabric and black trims are perfect for that rockabilly look.

Cutting and marking

Trace the required pattern pieces onto tissue paper (see page 90) and cut out. Pin the paper pattern pieces to your chosen fabric and cut out, remembering to transfer all reference marks to the fabric pieces (see page 90). Re-using the paper patterns, cut out the required pieces of interfacing. Following the manufacturer's instructions, apply them to the wrong side of their fabric counterparts.

Shirt

1   Draw your name, or print it out on your computer. Place the patch pocket fabric on the drawing or computer printout and trace around the name with a hard pencil. Fill in the name, using satin stitch (see page 91). (Alternatively, use ink jet transfer print paper to create a printed emblem.)

2   Place the pocket band on the wrong side of the pocket, aligning the raw edges. Pin in place, and stitch to join. Press the seam allowance toward the pocket. Fold the raw edge of the pocket band over to the wrong side by ⅜ in. (1 cm) and press the edge. Fold the pocket band over to the right side of the pocket, pin in place, and topstitch using a contrasting color of thread.

You will need

3¼ yd (3 m) polka-dot fabric, 56 in. (144 cm) wide

1 yd (90 cm) black contrast fabric, 56 in. (144 cm) wide

1 yd (90 cm) lightweight iron-on interfacing, 1 yd (90 cm) wide

60 in. (150 cm) elastic, 1 in. (2.5 cm) wide

8 x ¾-in. (18-mm) buttons

Red embroidery floss (thread)

Red contrast sewing thread

Sewing machine

Needle and matching sewing threads

Fabric pattern pieces required

Shirt

Polka-dot fabric: Left and right front panels, back panel, left and right sleeves, 1 patch pocket

Black fabric: Left and right front panel facings, back neck facing, 2 collars, 2 cuff bands, 1 pocket band

Interfacing: Left and right front panel facings, back neck facing, 2 collars

Pants

Polka-dot fabric: Left front and back legs, right front and back legs, 1 patch pocket

Black fabric: 2 hem bands, 1 pocket band

Take ½-in. (1.5-cm) seam allowances throughout unless otherwise stated.

3 Using a card template, press under the side and bottom edges of the pocket (see page 92). Pin the pocket to the right front of the shirt and topstitch in place, stitching as close to the edge of the pocket as possible.

4 With right sides together, stitch the front panels to the back panel at the shoulders. Overlock or zigzag stitch the raw edges together and press the seams toward the front.

5 Make the collar and attach the facings (see page 92). When pressing the front edge, allow the facing to roll over to the front by ⅟₁₆ in. (1 mm).

6 With right sides together, matching the balance marks, pin the right sleeve to the right armhole. Stitch the seam, overlock or zigzag stitch the raw edges together, and press toward the sleeve. Repeat for the left sleeve.

7 Match up the underarm and side seam edges and pin in place. Stitch from cuff to hem, overlock or zigzag stitch the edges together, and press the seams toward the front.

8 To finish the cuffs, first make an inverted pleat on the sleeves. Mark the center of each sleeve with a pin. Snip a notch ½ in. (1.5 cm) away from the pin on either side.

9 Folding the fabric right sides together, match the notches up and stitch a small tack to hold in place.

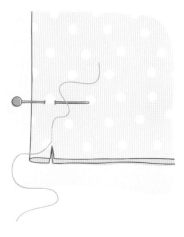

10 Distribute the pleat evenly on both sides of the tack. Stitch to hold in place.

11

With right sides together, stitch the short edges of each cuff band together to make a loop. Press the seams open. With wrong sides together, matching the raw edges, fold each cuff band in half widthwise and press the edge. Place the cuff band on the sleeve, aligning the raw edges. Pin and stitch in place. Overlock or zigzag stitch the raw edges together and press toward the sleeve. Topstitch, using a contrasting color of thread.

12 Overlock or zigzag stitch the raw edge at the hem. With the facing and shirt right sides together, stitch along the hem on the facing taking a 1⅛-in. (3-cm) seam allowance. Turn right side out and push the corners out. Fold the raw edge of the facing over by 1⅛ in. (3 cm), press, pin, and stitch in place using a contrasting color of thread. Topstitch along the whole front edge, using contrasting thread.

13 Mark the position of the buttonholes along the right center front and stitch, using contrasting thread (see page 94). Sew buttons along the left center front to correspond with the buttonholes, and at the pleats on the cuffs.

Pants

1 First make the pocket. Place the pocket band on the wrong side of the pocket, aligning the raw edges. Pin in place and stitch to join. Press the seam allowance toward the pocket. Fold the raw edge of the pocket band over to the wrong side by ⅜ in. (1cm) and press the edge. Fold the pocket band over to the right side of the pocket, pin in place, and topstitch using a contrasting color of thread. Pin the pocket to the right back and topstitch in place, stitching as close to the edge of the pocket as possible.

2 Overlock or zigzag stitch the inside and outside legs and crotch. Assemble the pants (see page 93), pressing all seams open as you go.

3 At the waist, fold the edge over by ⅜ in. (1 cm) and then again by 1⅛ in. (3 cm). Press, pin, and stitch in place, stopping 1½ in. (4 cm) away from the top edge at the center back. Attach a safety pin to one end of the elastic and thread it through the waist channel. Remove the safety pin. Hand stitch the ends of the elastic together. Hand stitch the gap at the center back closed.

4 Snip a notch ½ in. (1.5 cm) away from the outside leg seam on each side and make an inverted pleat, as in Steps 8 and 9 of the Shirt.

5 With right sides together, stitch the short edges of each hem band together to make a loop. Press the seams open. With wrong sides together, aligning the raw edges, fold each hem band in half widthwise and press the edge. Place the hem band on the leg, aligning the raw edges. Pin and stitch in place. Overlock or zigzag stitch the raw edges together and press the seam allowance toward the leg. Topstitch using a contrasting thread. Sew a button onto each leg at the base of the inverted pleats.

Ocean Breeze

This pretty tunic top and matching pants are ideal for lounging around on a lazy summer morning. The broderie anglaise contrast details, gold crochet trim, and cute buttons give the design a delicate, feminine look.

Cutting and marking

Trace the required pattern pieces onto tissue paper and cut out (see page 90). Pin the paper pattern pieces on your chosen fabric and cut out, remembering to transfer all reference marks to the fabric pieces (see page 90). Do not cut the neckline keyhole slit.

Shirt

1   Stay stitch ⅜ in. (1 cm) in from the neckline edges of the front and back panels to prevent stretching. With right sides together, machine stitch the front and back pieces together at the shoulders. Overlock or zigzag stitch the raw edges together, and press the seams toward the front. With right sides together, machine stitch the front and back facings together at the shoulders and press the seams open.

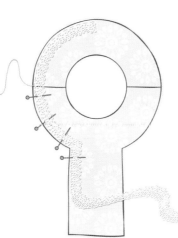

2   With right sides together, align the edge of the crochet trim with the outer edge of the facing. Pin in place and machine stitch, taking a ¼-in. (0.5-cm) seam allowance. Press the seam toward the facing.

You will need

3¾ yd (3.5 m) solid (plain) fabric, 56 in. (144 cm) wide

24 in. (60 cm) contrast trim fabric, 56 in. (144 cm) wide

5½ yd (5 m) crochet trim, 1 in. (2.5 cm) wide

1¾ yd (1.5 m) elastic, 1 in. (2.5 cm) wide

5 x ¼-in. (7-mm) buttons

Sewing machine

Needle and matching sewing threads

Fabric pattern pieces required
Shirt
Solid (plain) fabric: Front panel (place on fold of fabric to cut 1 piece), back panel, left and right sleeves

Contrast trim fabric: Front neck facing, back neck facing, tie belt, 2 belt loops, 2 cuff bands, 1 hem band

Pants
Main fabric: Left front and back legs, right front and back legs

Contrast trim fabric: 2 hem bands

Take ½-in. (1.5-cm) seam allowances throughout unless otherwise stated.

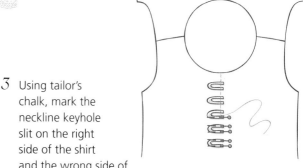

3   Using tailor's chalk, mark the neckline keyhole slit on the right side of the shirt and the wrong side of the facing. Cut a 12 x ⅜-in. (30 x 2-cm) bias strip of the solid (plain) fabric and make a rouleau (see page 94). Cut the rouleau into five 1½-in. (4-cm) lengths. Fold each piece into a loop and pin them in place ½ in. (1.5 cm) apart along the keyhole slit line on the right side of the shirt. Machine stitch down the slit line to attach the loops.

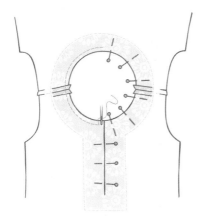

4

With the right side of the facing against the wrong side of the shirt, pin the facing in place around the neckline of the shirt and down the keyhole slit line. Starting at the center back, machine stitch along the neckline. Stop with the needle down ¼ in. (0.5 cm) before the slit line, turn the work around, and start stitching along the slit line.

5

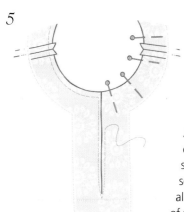

About 2 in. (5 cm) before the end of slit line, reduce the stitch length to reinforce the seam and narrow the seam allowance to nothing at the end of the slit. Stop with the needle down, turn the work around, and stitch up the other side of the slit line.

6 Cut down the slit line, stopping just below the point. Trim the seam allowances along the neckline to ¼ in. (0.5 cm). Turn the shirt right side out, so that the facing is on the front, and press the neckline edge. Pin the trimmed facing edge in place on the front of the shirt and topstitch. Sew buttons onto the opposite side of the shirt to correspond with the rouleaux loops.

7 With right sides together, matching the balance marks, pin the right sleeve to the right armhole (see page 93). Stitch the seam, overlock or zigzag stitch the raw edges together, and press toward the sleeve. Repeat for the left sleeve. Match up the underarm and side seam edges and pin in place. Stitch from cuff to hem, overlock or zigzag stitch the edges together, and press the seams toward the front.

8

Cut a piece of crochet trim to the same length as the cuff band. Machine stitch the short edges of the trim together to make a loop. With right sides together, machine stitch the short edges of each cuff band together, and press the seams open. With wrong sides together, aligning the raw edges, fold each cuff band in half widthwise, and press. Pin the trim in place along the raw edge of the cuff band and stitch in place, taking a ¼-in. (0.5-cm seam) allowance. With right sides together, aligning the raw edges and sandwiching the trim between the sleeve and the cuff band, pin the cuff band in place on the sleeve. Stitch in place. Overlock or zigzag stitch the raw edges together, and press toward the cuff.

9 Fold each belt loop piece in half widthwise and press. Open out, fold in each long edge to meet the creased center mark, and press. Fold in half again, aligning the folded edges. Pin along the edge, and machine stitch in place. Fold over ⅜ in. (1 cm) at each short end of the loop and press. Pin one loop onto the shirt at each side seam and stitch in place.

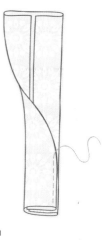

10 With right sides together, aligning the raw edges, fold the belt piece in half widthwise. Machine stitch along one short edge and the long raw edge, leaving one short edge open. Turn the belt right side out and press the edges flat. Tuck the raw edges into the open end of the belt and hand stitch to close.

Pants

1 Overlock or zigzag stitch the inside and outside legs and crotch, leaving the top edges and hems unfinished. Measure the outside leg length and cut two pieces of crochet trim to this measurement. Assemble the pants (see page 93), pressing all seams open as you go. When stitching the outside leg seams, sandwich the crochet trim between the front and back leg pieces.

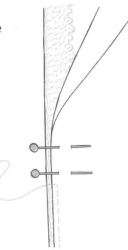

2 At the waist, fold the edge over to the wrong side by ⅜ in. (1 cm) and then again by 1⅛ in. (3 cm). Press, pin, and stitch in place, stopping 1½ in. (4 cm) away from the top edge at the center back. Attach a safety pin to one end of the elastic and thread it through the waist channel. Remove the safety pin. Hand stitch the ends of the elastic together. Hand stitch the gap at the center back closed.

3 Cut a piece of crochet trim to the same length as the hem band. Machine stitch the short edges of the trim together to make a loop. With right sides together, machine stitch the short edges of each hem band together, and press the seams open. With wrong sides together, aligning the raw edges, fold each hem band in half widthwise, and press. Pin the trim in place along the raw edge of the hem band and stitch in place, taking a ¼-in. (0.5-cm) seam allowance. With right sides together, aligning the raw edges and sandwiching the trim between the leg and the hem band, pin the hem band in place on the leg. Stitch in place. Overlock or zigzag stitch the raw edges together, and press toward the hem.

Floral Bouquet

These cute summer pajamas are full of lovely details, including ruffles on the sleeves and hems and yellow bias-binding trim. Use pretty floral prints in different colors, and then finish the shirt off with bright purple buttons for a cheery touch!

Cutting and marking

Trace the required pattern pieces onto tissue paper (see page 90) and cut out. Pin the paper pattern pieces to your chosen fabric and cut out, remembering to transfer all reference marks to the fabric pieces (see page 90). Re-using the paper patterns, cut out the required pieces of interfacing and apply them to the wrong side of their fabric counterparts.

Shirt

1 Trim the seam allowance on the patch pocket pieces by ⅜ in. (1 cm) along the side and bottom edges, leaving the top edge as it is. Open out the bias binding and pin it around the side and bottom edges of the wrong side of the pocket. Stitch along the crease in the binding.

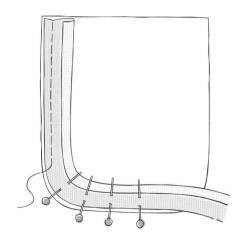

2

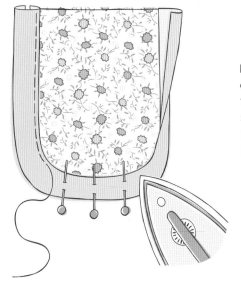

Fold the binding over to the right side of the pocket and press it flat. Leave the bias binding folded along the second crease mark. Pin it in place, and topstitch along the inside edge of the binding.

3 Fold the top edge of the pocket over to the wrong side by 1⅛ in. (3 cm). Press the edge, pin, and topstitch in place.

You will need

2¼ yd (200 cm) yellow floral fabric, 56 in. (144 cm) wide

2¼ yd (200 cm) purple floral fabric, 56 in. (144 cm) wide

36 in. (90 cm) lightweight iron-on interfacing, 36 in. (90 cm) wide

60 in. (150 cm) elastic, 1 in. (2.5 cm) wide

4 x ⅝-in. (15 mm) buttons

5½ yd (500 cm) yellow cotton bias binding 1 in. (2.5 cm)

Sewing machine

Needle and matching sewing threads

Fabric pattern pieces required

Shirt

Yellow floral fabric: Left and right front panels, back panel, left and right sleeves

Purple floral fabric: Left and right front panel facings, back neck facing, 2 collars, 2 cuff bands, 2 patch pockets

Interfacing: Left and right front panel facings, back neck facing, 2 collars

Shorts

Yellow floral fabric: Left front and back legs, right front and back legs

Purple floral fabric: 2 hem bands

Take ½-in. (1.5-cm) seam allowances throughout unless otherwise stated.

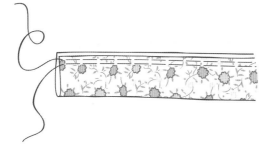

4

Now make the pocket ruffle. Cut two 3 x 32-in. (8 x 80-cm) strips of contrast fabric for the pocket ruffles. Fold each strip in half widthwise, with wrong sides together, and press the edge. Run a gathering stitch (see page 94) along the raw edge of each strip.

5 Pull the threads to gather each ruffle to about 16 in. (40 cm) in length, spreading the gathers evenly. Pin the pockets right side up on top of the ruffles, with the folded edges of the ruffles facing outward, making sure that the gathering stitching is hidden underneath the pockets. At the top of each pocket, fold the ruffle edges over to the wrong side to hide the raw edges. Pin the pockets in place on the fronts of the shirt. Topstitch along the outside edge of the bias binding to attach the pockets to the shirt.

6 With right sides together, machine stitch the front panels to the back panel at the shoulders. Overlock or zigzag stitch the edges together, and press the seam allowances toward the front. Attach the collar and facings (see page 92).

7 With right sides together, matching the balance marks, pin the right sleeve to the right armhole (see page 93). Stitch the seam, overlock or zigzag stitch the raw edges together, and press toward the sleeve. Repeat for the left sleeve. Match up the underarm and side seam edges and pin in place. Stitch from cuff to hem, overlock or zigzag stitch the edges together, and press the seams toward the front.

8 With right sides together, stitch the short edges of each cuff band together to make a loop. Press the seams open. With wrong sides together, aligning the raw edges, fold each cuff band in half widthwise and press the edge. Pin the cuff bands on the sleeves, aligning the raw edges, and stitch in place. Overlock or zigzag stitch the raw edges together and press the seam allowances toward the sleeves.

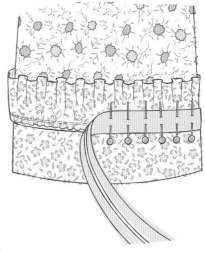

9 To make the sleeve ruffles, measure the sleeve circumference and double that measurement. Cut two strips to that length and 3 in. (8 cm) deep. Fold each ruffle piece in half widthwise, with wrong sides together, and press the edge. Run a gathering stitch (see page 94) along the raw edge and gather the ruffle up by half, spreading the gathers evenly. Aligning the gathered edge of the ruffle with the seam between the sleeve and the cuff band, pin the ruffle on the sleeve, and stitch in place. Pin bias binding on top of the ruffle to cover the stitching and raw edges. Topstitch along both edges of the binding to attach.

10 Overlock or zigzag stitch the raw edge at the hem. With the facing and shirt right sides together, stitch along the hem on the facing taking a 1⅛-in. (3-cm) seam allowance. Turn right side out and push the corners out. Fold the raw edge of the facing over by 1⅛ in. (3 cm), press, pin, and stitch in place, using a contrasting color thread. Topstitch along the whole front edge, using a contrasting color thread.

11 Mark the position of the buttonholes along the right center front and stitch (see page 94). Sew buttons along the left center front to correspond.

Shorts

1 Overlock or zigzag stitch the inside and outside legs and crotch. Assemble the shorts (see page 93), pressing all seams open as you go.

2 At the waist, fold the edge over to the wrong side by ⅜ in. (1 cm) and then again by 1⅛ in. (3 cm). Press, pin, and stitch in place, stopping 1½ in. (4 cm) away from the top edge at the center back. Attach a safety pin to one end of the elastic and thread it through the waist channel. Remove the safety pin. Hand stitch the ends of the elastic together. Hand stitch the gap at the center back closed.

3 With right sides together, machine stitch the short edges of each hem band together to make a loop. Press the seams open. With wrong sides together, aligning the raw edges, fold each hem band in half widthwise and press the edge. Aligning the edges, pin the hem bands on the legs, and machine stitch in place. Overlock or zigzag stitch the raw edges together and press the seam allowances toward the legs.

4 To make the hem ruffles, measure the hem circumference and double that measurement. Cut two strips to that length and 3 in. (8 cm) deep. Fold each ruffle piece in half widthwise, with wrong sides together, and press the edge. Run a gathering stitch (see page 94) along the raw edge and gather the ruffle up by half, spreading the gathers evenly. Aligning the gathered edge of the ruffle with the seam between the leg and the hem band, pin the ruffle on the hem, and stitch in place. Pin bias binding on top of the ruffle to cover the stitching and raw edges. Topstitch along both edges of the binding to attach.

Sunset Boulevard

These luxurious satin pajamas simply ooze old-school Hollywood glamour. Wear this elegant pair to bed and feel like you could be spending the night in the Chateau Marmont or the Hollywood Roosevelt—so chic!

Cutting and marking

Trace the required pattern pieces onto tissue paper (see page 90) and cut out. Pin the paper pattern pieces to your chosen fabric and cut out, remembering to transfer all reference marks to the fabric pieces (see page 90). Re-using the paper patterns, cut out the required pieces of interfacing and apply to the wrong side of their fabric counterparts.

Shirt

1   For the breast pocket, lay the lace pocket piece on top of the main fabric pocket piece. Pin in place and machine stitch, taking a ¼-in. (0.5-cm) seam. Fold the top edge of the pocket over by 1⅛ in. (3 cm) and press the edge. Using a card template, press under the side and bottom edges of the pocket (see page 92). Pin the pocket to the right front of the shirt and stitch in place, stitching as close to the edge as possible.

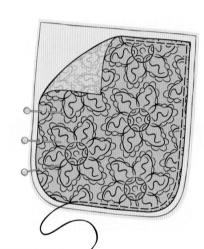

2   With right sides together, stitch the front panels to the back panel at the shoulders. Overlock or zigzag stitch the raw edges together, and press the seams toward the front.

You will need

3¾ yd (3.5 m) satin fabric, 56 in. (144 cm) wide

12 in. (30 cm) black lace, 56 in. (144 cm) wide

1 yd (100 cm) black contrast fabric, 56 in. (144 cm) wide

36 in. (90 cm) lightweight iron-on interfacing, 36 in. (90 cm) wide

4½ yd (4 m) ⅛-in. (4-mm) piping cord

1¾ yd (1.5 m) black satin ribbon, 1⅛ in. (3 cm) wide

4 x ¾-in. (2-cm) self-covering buttons

Sewing machine

Needle and matching sewing threads

Fabric pattern pieces required

Shirt
Satin fabric: Left and right front panels, left and right front panel facings, back panel, back neck facing, left and right sleeves, 2 collars, 1 patch pocket, 2 cuff bands

Lace: 2 cuff bands, 1 patch pocket

Interfacing: Left and right front panel facings, back neck facing, 2 collars

Pants
Satin fabric: Left front and back legs, right front and back legs, 2 hem bands

Lace: 2 hem bands

Take ½-in. (1.5-cm) seam allowances throughout unless otherwise stated.

3 From the contrast fabric, cut
five bias strips measuring
40 x 1⅛ in. (100 x 3 cm). Join
the bias strips together to get
one long piece (see page 94).
Place the piping cord in the
center of the bias strip and
fold the edges over, trapping
the cord inside.

4 With right sides together,
aligning the raw edges,
sandwich the bias strip in
between the two collar
pieces and pin in place.
Machine stitch, using a
half-presser foot to get
the stitching very close to
the piping cord.

5 Now attach the facings
(see page 92). Insert
piping along the front
edges, in the same way as
for the collar, up to the
point where the collar
joins the facing.

6 With right sides together, matching the balance marks,
pin the right sleeve to the right armhole (see page 93).
Stitch the seam, overlock or zigzag stitch the raw edges
together, and press toward the sleeve. Repeat for the left
sleeve.

7 Match up the underarm and side seam edges and pin in
place. Stitch from cuff to hem, overlock or zigzag stitch the
raw edges together, and press the seams toward the front.

8 Lay the lace cuff band on top of the fabric one. Pin together
and machine stitch around all four edges, taking a ¼-in.
(0.5-cm) seam allowance. With right sides together,
machine stitch the short edges of each cuff band together
to make a loop. Press the seams open. With wrong sides
together, aligning the raw edges, fold each cuff band in half
widthwise, and press.

9 Measure the cuff
circumference,
add 1½ in. (4 cm),
and cut a piece
of piping cord
and a bias strip
to this measurement. Place the piping cord in the center of
the bias strip and fold the edges over, trapping the cord
inside. Aligning the raw edges, pin the piping on the sleeve.
With right sides together, aligning the raw edges, pin the
cuff band on the sleeve, sandwiching the piping between
the sleeve and cuff band. Machine stitch, using a half-
presser foot. Overlock or zigzag stitch the raw edges
together and press the seam allowance toward the sleeve.

10 Overlock or zigzag stitch the raw edge of the hem. With the
facing and shirt right sides together, stitch along the hem on
the facing, taking a 1⅛-in. (3-cm) seam allowance. Turn
right side out and push the corners out. Fold the hem edge
over to the wrong side by 1⅛ in. (3 cm), press, pin, and
stitch in place.

11 Mark the position of the buttonholes along the right center
front and stitch (see page 94). Following the manufacturer's
instructions, cover the buttons with the main fabric and
with lace. Sew the buttons along the left center front to
correspond with the buttonholes.

Pants

1 Overlock or zigzag stitch the inside and outside legs and crotch. Assemble the pants (see page 93), pressing all seams open as you go. At the center front, leave a 1⅛-in. (3-cm) opening in the seam 1½ in. (4 cm) down from the top edge.

2 At the waist, fold the edge over to the wrong side by ⅜ in. (1 cm) and then by another 1⅛ in. (3 cm). Press, pin, and stitch in place. Attach a safety pin to one end of the black satin ribbon and thread it through the waist channel.

3 Lay the lace hem band on top of the fabric one. Pin together and machine stitch around all four edges, taking a ¼-in. (0.5-cm) seam allowance. With right sides together, machine stitch the short edges of each hem band together to make a loop. Press the seams open. With wrong sides together, aligning the raw edges, fold each hem band in half widthwise, and press.

4 Measure the hem circumference, add 1½ in. (4 cm), and cut a piece of piping cord and a bias strip to this measurement. Place the piping cord in the center of the bias strip and fold the edges over, trapping the cord inside. Aligning the raw edges, pin the piping on the leg. With right sides together, aligning the raw edges, pin the hem band on the leg, sandwiching the piping between the leg and hem band. Machine stitch, using a half-presser foot to get very close to the piping cord. Overlock or zigzag stitch the raw edges together and press the seam allowance toward the leg.

Blue Lagoon

Satin ribbon ties and a broderie anglaise trim add a hint of femininity to this stunning sleep set fashioned in deep, hypnotic blue.

Cutting and marking

Trace the required pattern pieces onto tissue paper (see page 90) and cut out. Pin the paper pattern pieces to your chosen fabric and cut out, remembering to transfer all reference marks to the fabric pieces (see page 90). Re-using the paper patterns, cut out the required pieces of interfacing and apply them to the wrong side of their fabric counterparts.

Shirt

1 Along the top edge of each pocket, fold over ½ in. (1.5 cm) to the wrong side and press. Lay a strip of broderie anglaise trim face up on the right side of the pocket, so that the bottom edge of the trim is ¾ in. (2 cm) below the upper edge of the pocket. Pin, baste (tack), and machine stitch in place. Fold under ½ in. (1.5 cm) around the remaining edges of the pockets, and press.

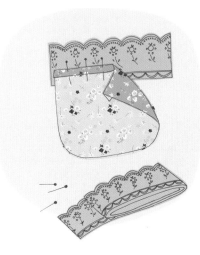

2 Stay stitch ⅜ in. (1 cm) in from the neckline edges of the front and back panels to prevent stretching. Pin a patch pocket to the right front panel, baste (tack), and machine stitch in place, stitching as close as possible to the pocket edges. Repeat for the left front panel.

3 With right sides together, machine stitch the front panels to the back panel at the shoulders. Overlock or zigzag stitch the edges together, and press the seam allowances toward the front. Attach the collar and facings (see page 92).

4 With right sides together, matching the balance marks, pin the right sleeve to the right armhole (see page 93). Stitch the seam, overlock or zigzag stitch the raw edges together, and press toward the sleeve. Repeat for the left sleeve.

5 Cut two 36-in. (90-cm) lengths of satin ribbon for the back waist ties and double hem one end of each. Pin the other end of each length to each side of the back panel at waist level, on the right side of the fabric, and secure with machine stitches. Match up the underarm and side seam edges and pin in place. Stitch from cuff to hem, overlock or zigzag stitch the edges together, and press the seams toward the front.

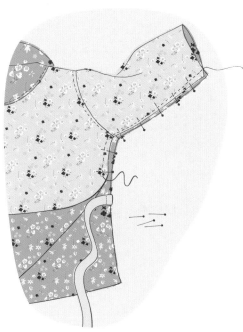

You will need

3 yd (3 m) floral print fabric, 56 in. (144 cm) wide

2¾ yd (240 cm) broderie anglaise/eyelet edging, 2 in. (5 cm) deep

3¾ yd (350 cm) satin ribbon, ½ in. (15mm) wide, for back waist ties and drawstring

12 in. (30 cm) lightweight iron-on interfacing, 36 in. (90 cm) wide

4 x ½-in. (15mm) buttons

Sewing machine

Needle and matching sewing threads

Fabric pattern pieces required

Shirt

Floral fabric: Left and right front panels, left and right front panel facings, back panel, back neck facing, 2 collars, left and right sleeves, 2 front patch pockets

Interfacing: Left and right front panel facings, back panel facing, 1 collar

Pants

Floral fabric: Left front and back legs, right front and back legs, 2 front patch pockets

Take ½-in. (1.5-cm) seam allowances throughout unless otherwise stated.

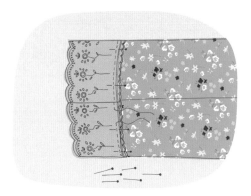

6 To finish the sleeves, fold the edges over to the wrong side by ½ in. (1.5 cm), and press. Cut two strips of broderie anglaise trim 1 in. (3 cm) longer than the circumference of the cuff. With right sides together, machine stitch the short ends together to form a loop. Press the seams open. Aligning the seams, pin the wrong side of one loop to the right side of one sleeve edge, so that the top edge of the trim is ¾ in. (2 cm) above the edge of the sleeve. Baste (tack), and machine stitch the trim in place. Repeat for the other sleeve.

7 Along the hem, fold under the edge by ⅜ in. (1 cm) and then by 1¼ in. (3 cm). Pin, baste (tack), and machine stitch in place.

8 Mark the position of the buttonholes along the right center front and stitch (see page 94). Sew buttons along the left center front to correspond.

Pants

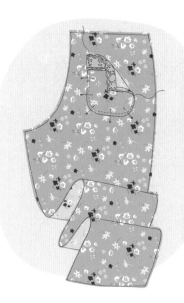

1 Pin the remaining patch pockets to the right and left front legs. Baste (tack) and machine stitch in place, stitching as close as possible to the pocket edges.

2 Overlock or zigzag stitch the inside and outside legs and crotch. Assemble the pants (see page 93), pressing all seams open as you go.

3 At the waist, fold the edge over to the wrong side by ⅜ in. (1 cm) and then again by 1⅛ in. (3 cm). Press the edge to make a crease line. Open the fold out again and mark the buttonhole positions on both sides, ½ in. (1.5 cm) down from the crease line and 1½ in. (4 cm) away from the center front. Make the buttonholes (see page 94). Pin the folded waist edge in place and stitch the waist channel.

4 Cut a 66-in. (170 cm) length of satin ribbon and double hem each end. Attach a safety pin to one end and thread the ribbon through the casing via the buttonholes. Remove the safety pin. To prevent the ribbon from unthreading, machine stitch through the casing at the center back seam.

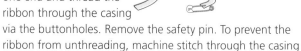

5 To finish the legs, fold the raw edges over to the wrong side by ½ in. (1.5 cm), and press. Cut two strips of broderie anglaise trim 1 in. (3 cm) longer than the circumference of the hem. With right sides together, machine stitch the short ends together to form a loop. Press the seams open. Aligning the seams, pin the wrong side of one loop to the right side of one leg edge, so that the top edge of the trim is ¾ in. (2 cm) above the edge of the leg. Baste (tack), and machine stitch the trim in place. Repeat for the other leg.

Sophisticated Sunday

Made in a bold geometric print, this belted kimono-style shirt is distinctively modern. You might even love it so much you want to wear it out of the house—team it with jeans and sneakers for the perfect weekend outfit!

Cutting and marking

Trace the required pattern pieces onto tissue paper (see page 90) and cut out. Pin the paper pattern pieces to your chosen fabric and cut out, remembering to transfer all reference marks to the fabric pieces (see page 90).

Shirt

1 With right sides together, machine stitch the fronts and back together at the shoulders. Overlock or zigzag stitch the raw edges together, and press the seams toward the front. With right sides together, fold the neckline band in half widthwise, and stitch along both short edges. Turn right side out, push out the corners, and press.

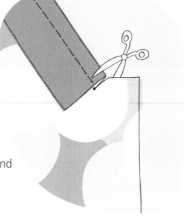

2 Pin the neckline band in place along the neckline, matching the notches. Machine stitch to join. Snip into the seam allowances to the balance mark, overlock or zigzag stitch the edges together, and press the seam toward the shirt.

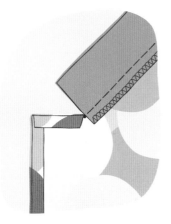

3 To finish the front edges, fold and press the seam allowances.

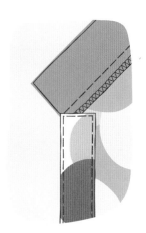

4 Pin in place and machine stitch.

You will need

2¼ yd (2 m) print cotton, 56 in. (144 cm) wide

2¼ yd (2 m) solid (plain) contrast fabric, 56 in. (144 cm) wide

1¾ yd (1.5 m) elastic, 1 in. (2.5 cm) wide

4½ yd (4 m) contrast ribbon, ½ in. (1.5 cm) wide

Sewing machine

Needle and matching sewing threads

Fabric pattern pieces required

Shirt

Print fabric: Left and right kimono front pieces, back kimono piece, left and right sleeves

Solid (plain) fabric: Neckline edge band, 2 belt pieces, 2 cuff bands

Pants

Print fabric: 2 hem bands

Solid (plain) fabric: Left front and back legs, right front and back legs

Take ½-in. (1.5-cm) seam allowances throughout unless otherwise stated.

5 With right sides together, matching the balance marks, pin the right sleeve to the right armhole (see page 93). Machine stitch the seam, overlock or zigzag stitch the raw edges together, and press toward the sleeve. Repeat for the left sleeve.

6 Match up the underarm and side seam edges and pin in place. Machine stitch from cuff to hem, overlock or zigzag stitch the raw edges together, and press the seams toward the front.

7 For the hem, fold the edge over to the wrong side by ⅜ in. (1 cm), and then by 1⅛ in. (3 cm) again, and press. Pin in place and topstitch to finish.

8
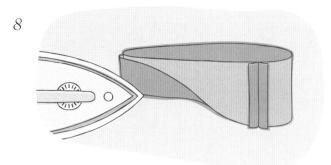

With right sides together, machine stitch the short edges of each cuff band together to make a loop. Press the seams open. Aligning the raw edges, with wrong sides together, fold each cuff band in half widthwise, and press. With right sides together, aligning the raw edges, pin the cuff band in place on the sleeve, and machine stitch in place. Overlock or zigzag stitch the raw edges together, and press the seam allowances toward the sleeve.

Pants

1 Overlock or zigzag stitch the raw side edges of the legs and crotch, leaving the top edges and hems unfinished.

2 With right sides together, stitch the left front leg to the left back leg along the outside leg seam. Repeat with the right front and back legs.

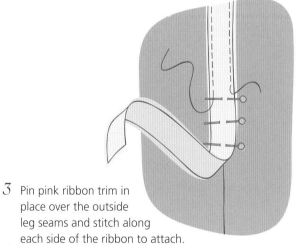

3 Pin pink ribbon trim in place over the outside leg seams and stitch along each side of the ribbon to attach.

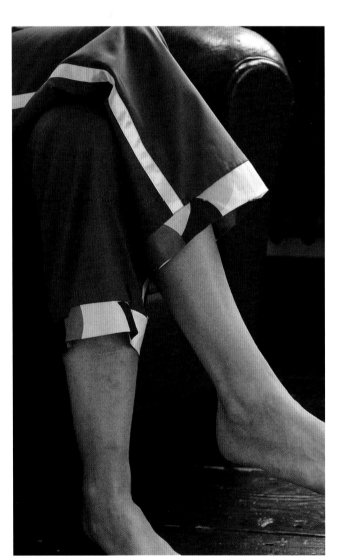

4 With right sides together, machine stitch the front and back legs together along the inside leg seam. Turn one leg right side out and put it inside the other leg. Matching the balance marks and inside leg seams, pin and machine stitch the crotch seam, stopping 1½ in. (4 cm) below the top edge at the center back to make an opening for the elastic. Press all seams open as you go.

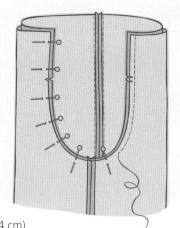

5 At the waist, fold the edge over to the wrong side by ⅜ in. (1 cm) and then again by 1⅛ in. (3 cm). Press, pin, and stitch in place, stopping 1½ in. (4 cm) away from the top edge at the center back. Attach a safety pin to one end of the elastic and thread it through the waist channel. Remove the safety pin. Hand stitch the ends of the elastic together. Hand stitch the gap at the center back closed.

6 With right sides together, machine stitch the short edges of each hem band together to form a loop. Press the seams open. With wrong sides together, aligning the raw edges, fold each hem band in half widthwise, and press. With right sides together, aligning the raw edges, pin the hem band in place on the leg, and stitch in place. Overlock or zigzag stitch the raw edges together, and press toward the hem.

Sleep Tight

A feminine take on the classic nightshirt, it is the choice of fabrics that makes this design so lovely. The bright red piping and buttons add a contemporary edge to the classic polka dots.

Cutting and marking

Trace the required pattern pieces onto tissue paper, add 9½ in. (24 cm) to the length of the shirt front and back pieces, and cut out. Pin the paper pattern pieces to your chosen fabric and cut out, remembering to transfer all reference marks to the fabric pieces (see page 90). Re-using the paper patterns, cut out the required pieces of interfacing. Following the manufacturer's instructions, apply them to the wrong side of their fabric counterparts.

Nightshirt

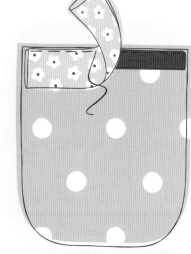

1 To make the breast pockets, cut two strips of red piping fabric the width of the pocket bands and 2 in. (5 cm) deep. Fold both pocket bands and piping strips in half widthwise, with wrong sides together, and press. Aligning the raw edges, lay the piping along the top edge of the pocket, pin, and stitch in place, taking a ¼-in. (0.5-cm) seam allowance. Place the pocket band on the top of the piping, pin in place, and stitch.

2 Press the seams toward the pocket band. Using a card template, press under the raw side and bottom edges of the pocket (see page 92). Pin the pocket to the right front of the shirt and topstitch in place, stitching as close to the edge of the pocket as possible.

3 With right sides together, stitch the front panels to the back panel at the shoulders. Overlock or zigzag stitch the edges together and press the seams toward the front. Make the collar and attach the facings (see page 92).

4 With right sides together, matching the balance marks, pin the right sleeve to the right armhole (see page 93). Stitch the seam, overlock or zigzag stitch the raw edges together, and press toward the sleeve. Repeat for the left sleeve.

5 Match up the underarm and side seam edges and pin in place. Stitch from cuff to hem, overlock or zigzag stitch the edges together, and press the seams toward the front.

6 Cut two piping strips the same length as the cuff bands and 2 in. (5 cm) deep. With right sides together, stitch the short edges of both cuff bands and piping strips to make them into loops. Press the seams open. Fold each cuff band and piping strip in half widthwise, wrong sides together, and press. Aligning the raw edges and seam joins, place a piping strip on each cuff band. Pin in place, and stitch, taking a ½-in. (0.5-cm) seam allowance.

You will need

2¾ yd (250 cm) polka-dot fabric, 54 in. (144 cm) wide

1¼ yd (100 cm) floral contrast fabric, 54 in. (144 cm) wide

8 in. (20 cm) red fabric for piping, 54 in. (144 cm) wide

36 in. (90 cm) lightweight iron-on interfacing, 36 in. (90 cm) wide

6 x ½-in. (15mm) buttons

Sewing machine

Needle and matching sewing threads

Fabric pattern pieces required

Polka-dot fabric: Left and right front panels, back panel, left and right sleeves, 2 patch pockets

Floral fabric: Left and right front panel facings, back neck facing, 2 collars, 2 cuff bands, 2 pocket bands

Interfacing: Left and right front panel facings, back neck facing, 2 collars

Take ½-in. (1.5-cm) seam allowances throughout unless otherwise stated.

7

Place the cuff bands on the sleeves, aligning the raw edges and sandwiching the piping between the cuff band and the sleeve. Pin and stitch in place. Overlock or zigzag stitch the raw edges together and press the seam allowance toward the cuff band. Topstitch, using a contrasting color of thread.

8

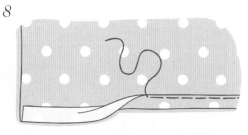

For the hem, fold the edge over to the wrong side by ⅜ in. (1 cm), and then by ⅜ in. (1 cm) again, and press. Pin in place, then machine stitch to finish.

9   Mark the position of the buttonholes along the right center front and stitch (see page 94). Sew buttons along the left center front to correspond.

Lovely Lace

For those occasions when you want to feel extra gorgeous, this lovely bias-cut camisole and matching boy shorts are faultless. The delicate lace trim adds a touch of luxury, and the satin fabric feels wonderful against the skin. Add a pretty bow and the feminine, sexy look is complete.

You will need

200 cm (2¼ yd) satin fabric, 56 in. (144 cm) wide

5½ yd (500 cm) ivory lace trim, 3 in. (8 cm) wide

1 yd (100 cm) ivory satin ribbon, 1½ in. (3.5 cm) wide

1½ yd (150 cm) elastic, 1 in. (2.5 cm) wide

Sewing machine

Needle and matching sewing threads

Fabric pattern pieces required

Camisole
Satin fabric: 2 pairs of bust panel, 1 front panel, 1 back panel, 1 back facing

Shorts
Satin fabric: Left front and back legs, right front and back legs

Take ½-in. (1.5-cm) seam allowances throughout unless otherwise stated.

Cutting and marking

Trace the required pattern pieces onto tissue paper (see page 90) and cut out. Pin the paper pattern pieces to your chosen fabric and cut out, remembering to transfer all reference marks to the fabric pieces (see page 90).

Camisole

1 Stitch the darts on all four bust panels (see page 92). Press the darts toward the side, away from the center front.

2

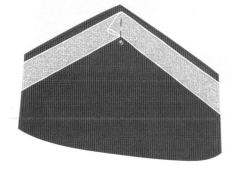

Cut a length of lace trim long enough to fit along the bust line and place it along the bust line of the front piece. At the center front, pinch a pleat on the lace trim to make it follow the angled bust line.

3

Place a pin to mark the end of the pleat. Stitch the pleat, trim the seam to ¼ in. (0.5 cm), and press the seam open.

4 Pin the lace trim along the bust line of the front piece. Stitch it in place, taking a ¼-in. (0.5-cm) seam allowance.

5

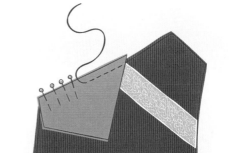

With right sides together, place one pair of bust panels on the front, aligning the raw edges. Pin in place and stitch, sandwiching the lace trim between the front and bust panels.

6 Overlock or zigzag stitch the edges together and press toward the bust panel.

7 The second pair of bust panels will be used as the front facing. With right sides together, machine stitch the second pair of bust panels together along the center front and press the seam open.

8 Overlock or zigzag stitch the side edges of the front and back pieces. With right sides together, stitch the front and back pieces together along the side seams, then press the seams open.

9 With right sides together, stitch the front and back facings together along the side seams. Press the seams open. Overlock or zigzag stitch the bottom edge of the facing.

10

Cut two 16 x ⅜-in. (40 x 2-cm) strips of satin fabric on the bias (see page 94). Make two long rouleaux (see page 94). Place the rouleaux on the camisole, pin, and stitch in place. With right sides together, lay the facing on top of the camisole. Pin in place and stitch, trapping the rouleaux straps between the body and the facing. Turn right side out and press the top edge. Baste (tack) the facing in place at the side seam.

11 Measure the hem circumference, add 1½ in. (3 cm), and cut a length of lace trim to this measurement. Stitch the short ends of the lace together, and press the seam open. Place the lace on the camisole, matching the edges and aligning the seam on the lace with the side seam. Pin in place, stitch, and press the seam toward the camisole. Topstitch.

12 Tie a bow from ivory satin ribbon. Hand stitch the bow to the center front of the camisole.

Shorts

1 Overlock or zigzag stitch the inside and outside legs and crotch. Assemble the shorts (see page 93), pressing all seams open as you go.

2 At the waist, fold the edge over to the wrong side by ⅜ in. (1 cm) and then again by 1⅛ in. (3 cm). Press, pin, and stitch in place, stopping 1½ in. (4 cm) away from the top edge at the center back. Attach a safety pin to one end of the elastic and thread it through the waist channel. Remove the safety pin. Hand stitch the ends of the elastic together. Hand stitch the gap at the center back closed.

3

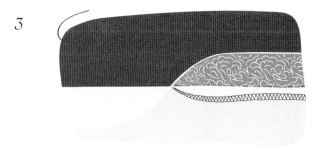

Measure the leg hem circumference, add 1 in. (3 cm), and cut two lengths of lace trim to this measurement. Stitch the short edges of each piece of lace together and press the seams open. Place the lace on the legs of the shorts, matching the edges and aligning the seam on the lace with the inside leg seam. Pin in place, stitch, and press the seams toward the shorts. Topstitch.

Nights in Satin

Ruffles and bows are used to great effect on this fun, flirty purple satin chemise. Choose a hot pink satin ribbon for a great color contrast. The flower corsage is detachable and would look equally lovely pinned to a favorite jacket.

You will need

2¼ yd (2 m) purple satin fabric, 56 in. (144 cm) wide

2¼ yd (2 m) hot pink satin ribbon, 1⅜ in. (3.5 cm) wide

2¼ yd (2 m) hot pink satin ribbon, ⅜ in. (1 cm) wide

Sewing machine

Needle and matching sewing threads

Fabric pattern pieces required

Satin fabric: 2 pairs of bust panel, 1 front panel, 1 back panel, 1 back facing

Take ½-in. (1.5-cm) seam allowances throughout unless otherwise stated.

Cutting and marking

Trace the required pattern pieces onto tissue paper (see page 90) and cut out. Pin the paper pattern pieces to your chosen fabric and cut out, remembering to transfer all reference marks to the fabric pieces (see page 90).

Chemise

1 Machine stitch the darts on all four bust panels (see page 92). Press the darts toward the side, away from the center front.

2 With right sides together, place one pair of bust panels on the front, aligning the raw edges. Pin in place and machine stitch. Overlock or zigzag stitch the edges together and press toward the bust panel.

3 The second pair of bust panels will be used as the front facing. With right sides together, machine stitch the second pair of bust panels together along the center front and press the seam open. With right sides together, machine stitch the front and back facings together along the side seams. Press the seams open. Overlock or zigzag stitch the bottom edge of the facing.

4 Overlock or zigzag stitch the side edges of the front and back pieces. With right sides together, machine stitch the front and back pieces together along the side seams, then press the seams open.

5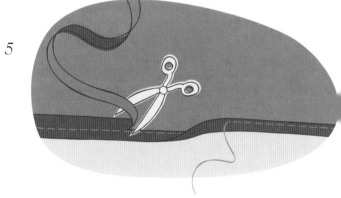

Cut two 2¾ x 27½-in. (7 x 70-cm) strips of purple satin for the straps. Fold one long edge over by about ¼ in. (0.5 cm) and machine stitch very close to the edge. Trim the seam allowance down to almost nothing, cutting as close as possible to the edge stitch line. Fold the edge over by as little as possible, giving a double fold around ⅟₁₆ in. (2mm) wide. Stitch along the edge again to finish the hem.

6

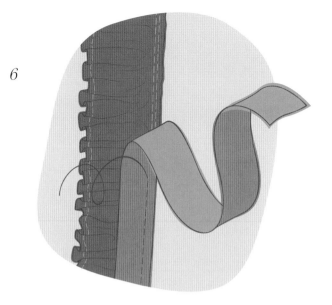

Run a gathering stitch along the other edge of each strip (see page 94). Gather to 13 in. (33 cm). Overlock or zigzag stitch the raw edges. Cut a 13-in. (33-cm) length of the wider satin ribbon. Place the ribbon on top of the ruffle, aligning the raw edge of the ruffle with the edge of the ribbon. Pin in place and machine stitch. Fold the ribbon over to cover the stitching and press.

7 Pin the straps on the body and machine stitch in place. Lay the facing on top of the body, right sides together. Pin it in place and machine stitch, trapping the straps between the body and the facing. Turn right side out and press the edge. Baste (tack) the facing to the seam allowance at the side seam.

8 Cut a 2¾ x 55-in. (7 x 140-cm) strip of purple satin for the hem ruffle. Make the hem ruffle in the same way as the straps, gathering the ruffle to the circumference of the hem. With right sides together, join the short edges of the ruffle to make a loop and press the seam open. With right sides together, aligning the raw edges, place the ruffle on the hem. Pin and machine stitch in place. Overlock or zigzag stitch the raw edges together and press toward the body.

9

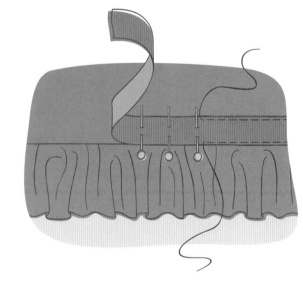

Starting at the side seam, pin the narrow ribbon over the seam between the body and the ruffle. Topstitch along both edges of the ribbon to attach.

10 From the remaining narrow ribbon, make two bows. Hand stitch one bow to the base of each strap on the front of the body.

11 To make the detachable corsage, cut a 12-in. (30-cm) length of wide ribbon and a 2¾ x 24-in. (7 x 60-cm) strip of purple satin fabric. Fold the fabric strip in half widthwise and press the edge. Run a gathering stitch (see page 94) along the raw edges and gather to 12 in. (30 cm). Lay the ribbon on top of the ruffle and machine stitch along the edge to join. Roll the ruffle up to create a corsage, hand stitching at the base as you go to hold the flower together. Once you have rolled the whole thing up, tie the thread off to secure. Sew a safety pin or brooch pin to the back of the corsage. Pin onto the center front at the bust.

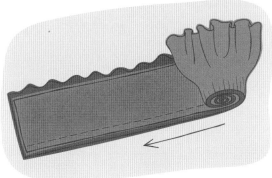

Plaid Pants

A classic plaid never goes out of style. This pair of pajama bottoms, made from soft cotton flannel, will keep you warm and cozy during cold winter nights and looks so flattering, too!

You will need

2¼ yd (200 cm) plaid cotton flannel fabric, 56 in. (144 cm) wide

60 in. (150 cm) cotton ribbon, ¾ in. (2 cm) wide

1 x ¾-in. (18-mm) button

Sewing machine

Needle and matching sewing threads

Fabric pattern pieces required

Cotton flannel fabric: Left front and back legs, right front and back legs, 2 fly facing pieces

Take ½-in. (1.5-cm) seam allowances throughout unless otherwise stated.

Cutting and marking

Trace the required pattern pieces onto tissue paper (see page 90) and cut out. Pin the paper pattern pieces to your chosen fabric and cut out, remembering to transfer all reference marks to the fabric pieces (see page 90).

Pants

1

Overlock or zigzag stitch the raw side edges of the legs and crotch, leaving the top edges and hems unfinished. Overlock or zigzag stitch all edges of the fly facing pieces. Place the fly facings on the front leg pieces at the center front, right sides together. Pin in place and machine stitch. Press the seam allowances toward the fly.

2

Machine stitch the left front leg to the left back leg along the inside leg seam. Repeat with the right front and back legs. With right sides together, aligning the balance marks and inside leg seams, pin and stitch the crotch seam from back to front, stopping at the front notch.

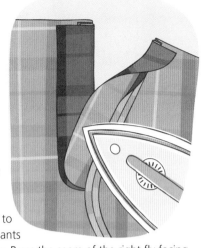

3   Press the crotch seam open. When you get to the fly facings, fold the left fly facing over to the inside of the pants and press the edge. Press the seam of the right fly facing piece open, so that it extends over to the left side.

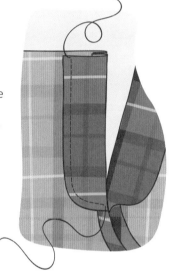

4   Pin the left fly facing in place and topstitch on the inside of the pants, following the edge of the fly facing along the bottom curve.

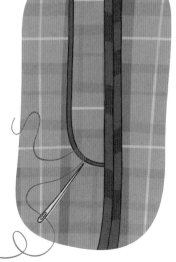

5   Hand stitch the right fly facing to the left fly facing at the curve to hold the facings in place.

6   To finish the hems, fold the edges over to the wrong side by ⅜ in. (1 cm) and then by 1⅛ in. (3 cm) and press the edge. Pin in place and machine stitch.

7

At the waist, fold the edge over to the wrong side by ⅜ in. (1 cm) and then again by 1⅛ in. (3 cm). Press the edge to make a crease line. Open the fold out again and mark the buttonhole positions on both sides, ½ in. (1.5 cm) down from the crease line and 1½ in. (4 cm) away from the center front. Make the buttonholes (see page 94).

8   Pin the folded waist edge in place and stitch the waist channel. Mark the buttonhole position on the left front at the center of the fly, ¾ in. (2 cm) down from the waist edge. Make the buttonhole and sew a button onto the right fly facing to correspond. Attach a safety pin to one end of the cotton ribbon and thread it through the waist channel buttonholes.

The Big Sleep

This is a modern take on classic men's pajamas. Large patch pockets and contrast piping are both traditional PJ details, but pairing the checked shirt with boxer shorts in a solid (plain) color gives the ensemble a fresh new look.

Cutting and marking

Trace the required pattern pieces onto tissue paper (see page 90) and cut out. Pin the paper pattern pieces to your chosen fabric and cut out, remembering to transfer all reference marks to the fabric pieces (see page 90). Re-using the paper patterns, cut out the required pieces of interfacing and apply them to the wrong side of their fabric counterparts.

Shirt

1 Fold the top edge of the patch pockets over to the wrong side by 1 in. (3 cm) and press the edge. Pin and machine stitch in place. Fold the side and bottom edges over to the wrong side by ½ in. (1.5 cm) and press. Pin the pockets in place on the body fronts and topstitch around the side and bottom edges, stitching as close to the edge as possible.

You will need

2¼ yd (200 cm) checked fabric, 56 in. (144 cm) wide

60 in. (150 cm) solid (plain) fabric, 56 in. (144 cm) wide

36 in. (90 cm) lightweight iron-on interfacing, 36 in. (90 cm) wide

60 in. (150 cm) elastic, 1 in. (2.5 cm) wide

6 x ¾-in. (18-mm) buttons

Sewing machine

Needle and matching sewing threads

Fabric pattern pieces required

Shirt
Checked fabric: Left and right front panels, left and right front panel facings, back panel, back neck facing, left and right sleeves, 2 large patch pockets, 4 pocket flaps

Shorts
Contrast fabric: Left front and back legs, right front and back legs

Take ½-in. (1.5-cm) seam allowances throughout unless otherwise stated.

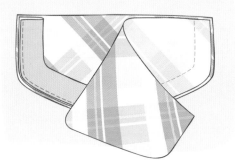

2 From the contrast fabric, cut two bias strips measuring 2 x 12 in. (5 x 30 cm) for the pocket piping details (see page 94). Fold each one in half widthwise and press the edge. Aligning the raw edges, pin each strip around the side and bottom edges of a pocket flap. Stitch in place, taking a ½-in. (1-cm) seam allowance. Pin a second pocket flap on top, right sides together, sandwiching the piping in between. Stitch in place. Trim the seam allowances to ¼ in. (0.5 cm), turn the flaps right side out, and press flat.

3

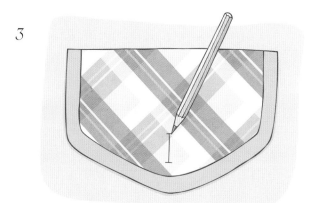

Mark and make a buttonhole on each pocket flap (see page 94).

4 Pin the pocket flaps onto the front body pieces ½ in. (1 cm) above each pocket, right sides together. Machine stitch to attach. Fold the pocket flaps over and press.

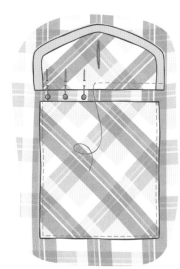

5 With right sides together, stitch the front panels to the back panel at the shoulders. Overlock or zigzag stitch the edges together and press the seam allowances toward the front.

6

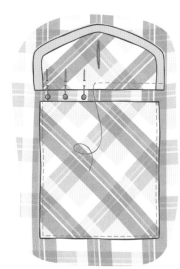

From the contrast fabric, cut a bias strip measuring 2 x 24 in. (5 x 60 cm) for the collar piping details. Make the collar (see page 92), sandwiching the piping strip between the two collar pieces in the same way as on the pocket flap.

7 Attach the facings (see page 92).

8 With right sides together, matching the balance marks, pin the right sleeve to the right armhole (see page 93). Stitch the seam, overlock or zigzag stitch the raw edges together, and press toward the sleeve. Repeat for the left sleeve. Match up the underarm and side seam edges and pin in place. Stitch from cuff to hem, overlock or zigzag stich the edges together, and press the seam allowances toward the front.

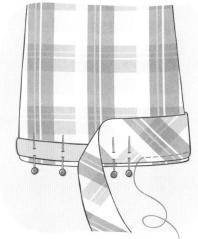

9 Cut a bias strip of contrast fabric the same length as the cuff band and 2 in. (5 cm) deep. With right sides together, stitch the short edges of both cuff band and piping strip together, and press the seams open. Fold each cuff band and piping strip in half widthwise, with wrong sides together, and press the edge. Aligning the raw edges and seams, pin the piping strip to the right side of the sleeve, with the cuff band right side down on top. Stitch in place, taking a ¼-in. (0.5-cm) seam allowance.

10 Overlock or zigzag stitch the raw edge at the hem. With the facing and shirt right sides together, stitch along the hem on the facing, taking a 1⅛-in. (3-cm) seam allowance. Turn right side out and push the corners out. Fold the remaining hem edge over to the wrong side by 1⅛ in. (3 cm), press, pin, and stitch.

11 Mark and make the buttonholes on the left center front (see page 94). Sew buttons along the right center front to correspond, and on the pockets.

Shorts

1 Overlock or zigzag stitch the inside and outside legs and crotch, leaving the top edges and hems untouched. Assemble the shorts (see page 93), pressing all seams open as you go.

2 At the waist, fold the edge over to the wrong side by ⅜ in. (1 cm) and then again by 1⅛ in. (3 cm). Press, pin, and stitch in place, using a contrasting color of thread, stopping 1½ in. (4 cm) away from the top edge at the center back. Attach a safety pin to one end of the elastic and thread it through the waist channel. Remove the safety pin. Hand stitch the ends of the elastic together. Hand stitch the gap at the center back closed.

3 To finish the hems, fold the edges over to the wrong side by ⅜ in. (1 cm) and then by another 1⅛ in. (3 cm). Press, pin, and topstitch using a contrasting color of thread.

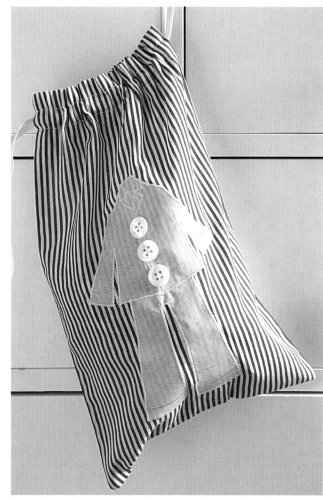

chapter 3

Bedtime bits and pieces

Cozy Cover

This stylish hot water bottle cover is quick and easy to sew, making it the perfect gift. The clever use of detail and trims, including the two-tone quilting stitch and the giant buttons, makes this project fun as well as functional.

Cutting and marking

Trace the required pattern pieces onto tissue paper (see page 90) and cut out. Pin the paper pattern pieces to your chosen fabric and cut out, remembering to transfer all reference marks to the fabric pieces (see page 90).

Cover

1 Start by marking guidelines for the quilting stitching on one of each of the fabric pieces. Using a ruler and tailor's chalk, lightly draw parallel diagonal lines across the fabric at 1½-in. (4-cm) intervals until the piece is covered. Now mark a second set of guidelines across the first ones, creating a grid.

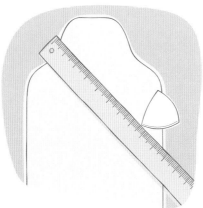

2 Sandwich the batting (wadding) between the two fabric pieces, with the marked piece on top. Pin all along the edges to hold the layers together. Machine stitch along the guidelines, using a twin needle threaded with two different colors of topstitching thread.

You will need

½ yd (50 cm) fabric, 56 in. (144 cm) wide

½ yd (50 cm) thin batting (wadding), 36 in (90 cm) wide

Topstitching thread in 2 colors

2 x 1⅛-in. (30-mm) buttons

Sewing machine

Needle and matching sewing threads

Twin needle

Fabric pattern pieces required

Fabric: 2 back pieces, 2 lower front pieces, 2 upper front pieces

Batting (wadding): 1 back piece, 1 lower front piece, 1 upper front piece

Take ½-in. (1.5-cm) seam allowances throughout unless otherwise stated.

3

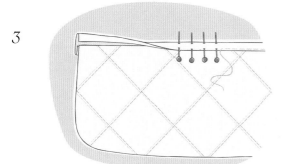

Cut two 1½ x 12-in. (4 x 30-cm) strips of fabric on the bias (see page 94). Fold each strip in half widthwise and press. Open out and fold each long edge in to meet the center crease line. With right sides together, pin one edge of the binding strip along the straight edge of the lower front. Machine stitch down the crease line. Fold the binding over to the right side, pin, and stitch close to the binding edge to finish. Repeat for the straight edge of the upper front piece.

4 Mark the position of the buttonholes on the lower front piece and stitch (see page 94). Sew buttons onto the upper front piece to correspond with the buttonholes.

5 Place the lower front piece on top of the back piece, right sides together. Place the upper front piece on top, creating an overlap. Pin and machine stitch all around the edges. Trim the seam allowance to ¼ in. (0.5 cm) and turn the cover right side out.

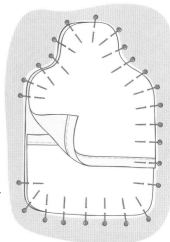

Night Owl

Relax after a stressful day with this gorgeous lavender-filled eye mask. The mask soothes tired eyes and the lovely scent ensures you drift off to sleep within minutes. And with these great fabrics and cute embroidery, it is perfectly pretty too!

Cutting and marking

Trace the required pattern pieces onto tissue paper (see page 90) and cut out. Pin the paper pattern pieces to your chosen fabric and cut out, remembering to transfer all reference marks to the fabric pieces (see page 90).

Mask

1   Write (or print on your computer) "Sweet dreams". Place one mask piece on the print-out and trace around the words, using a hard pencil. Alternatively, use ink jet transfer print paper to create a printed emblem. Using pink embroidery floss (thread), backstitch over the words.

You will need

12 in. (30 cm) solid (plain) fabric, 56 in. (144 cm) wide

8 in. (20 cm) striped fabric, 56 in. (144 cm) wide

Pink embroidery floss (thread)

10 oz (300 ml) rice

2 tablespoons dried lavender

Sewing machine

Needle and matching sewing threads

Fabric pattern pieces required

Solid (plain) fabric: 2 mask pieces

Take ½-in. (1.5-cm) seam allowances throughout unless otherwise stated.

2

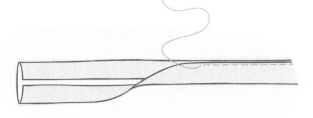

Cut two 3 x 13¾-in. (8 x 35-cm) strips of solid (plain) fabric for the ties. Fold each strip in half widthwise and press. Open out the strip and fold each long edge in to meet the center crease line. Press. Fold over again along the center crease line, pin in place, and machine stitch close to the edge to finish.

3   Cut a 2¾ x 47-in. (7 x 120-cm) strip of striped fabric for the frill. Fold the strip in half widthwise and press. Run a gathering stitch along the raw edges (see page 94). Gather the frill to 24 in. (60 cm).

4. Pin the frill on the embroidered mask piece, aligning the raw edges, and machine stitch. Place the straps on the other mask piece, lining them up inside the double notches at the sides. Pin and stitch in place. With right sides together, lay one mask piece on top of the other one, pin in place, and stitch along the edge, sandwiching the frill and ties between the two layers of fabric and leaving a 3-in. (8-cm) opening at the top.

5. Trim the seam allowance to ¼ in. (0.5 cm), then turn the mask right side out. Mix the lavender and rice together in a bowl. Using a funnel, pour the rice and lavender into the mask through the hole at the top. Fold in the edges at the opening, pin in place, and hand stitch to close the mask, making small, tight stitches to prevent any rice grains from falling out.

Keepin' Clean

This simple drawstring PJ case is an easy way to encourage kids to keep their bedroom tidy! Customize it by adding a groovy 3-D appliqué: contrast stitching and real shirt buttons help to make the appliqué stand out from the background.

You will need

20 in. (50 cm) striped fabric, 56 in. (144 cm) wide

Scrap of contrast fabric for appliqué

8 in. (20 cm) fusible bonding web, 17 in. (43 cm) wide

2¼ yd (2 m) yellow cotton cord

3 x ⅞-in. (22-mm) buttons

Yellow and white sewing thread

Sewing machine

Needle

Take ½-in. (1.5-cm) seam allowances throughout unless otherwise stated.

Cutting and marking

From the striped fabric, cut two pieces of fabric measuring 16 x 11 in. (42 x 28 cm) for the front and back pieces for the bag. Following the manufacturer's instructions, iron fusible bonding web onto the back of the contrast fabric. Using the pajama template on page 95, transfer the design onto the backing paper and cut it out. Peel the backing paper off the bonding web, place the pajama appliqué in the center of one of the striped pieces, and iron to fuse the fabrics together.

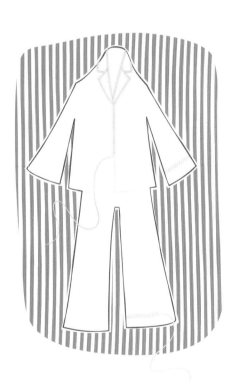

Drawstring bag

1 Using a hard pencil, draw the appliqué collar detailing on the pajama. Using a very short, narrow zigzag stitch and white thread, machine stitch to cover the pencil line. Change to a yellow contrast thread and zigzag stitch a line across each leg and sleeve to create the striped detail. Now change back to white thread and go all around the pajama outline, covering the raw fabric edges with narrow zigzag stitching.

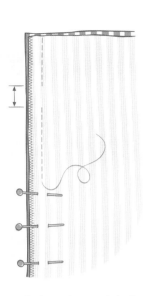

2 Overlock or zigzag stitch the
   sides and bottom edges of
   each striped piece separately.
   Lay one on top of the other,
   with right sides together, and
   pin along the side and bottom
   edges. Machine stitch to join
   the pinned edges, leaving a
   ¾-in. (2-cm) gap about 3 in.
   (8 cm) down from the top
   edge on both sides. Turn the
   bag right side out and press
   the edges.

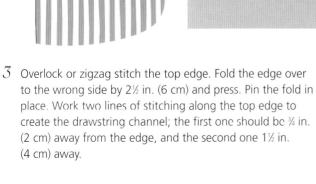

3 Overlock or zigzag stitch the top edge. Fold the edge over
   to the wrong side by 2½ in. (6 cm) and press. Pin the fold in
   place. Work two lines of stitching along the top edge to
   create the drawstring channel; the first one should be ¾ in.
   (2 cm) away from the edge, and the second one 1½ in.
   (4 cm) away.

4 Cut the piece of yellow cord in half. Using a safety pin,
   thread each piece of cord through the channel in opposite
   directions. Tie the ends of each piece of cord with a knot.

5 Sew three buttons onto the appliqué pajama shirt.

Kasbah Slippers

What a pretty way to keep your feet warm! These sequin-covered wool felt slippers add a touch of glamor even when you're lounging around the house. We've included patterns for both adult and children's sizes, so why not make matching pairs for mother and daughter?

Cutting and marking

Trace the required pattern pieces onto tissue paper (see page 90) and cut out. Pin the paper pattern pieces to your chosen fabric and cut out, remembering to transfer all reference marks to the fabric pieces (see page 90).

Slippers

1 Mark the seam allowance by sewing a hand basting (tacking) stitch line on each upper piece, ½ in. (1.5 cm) away from the edge. Cover the whole area inside the stitched line with sequins, arranging them in a random pattern. Tie off all threads on the wrong side of the fabric.

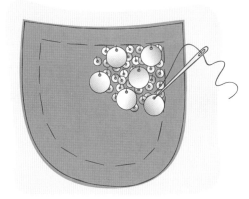

2 Lay a light pink upper piece on top of the beaded piece and pin along the straight edge. Machine stitch to join, turn right side out, and press the edge, being careful not to damage the sequins.

3
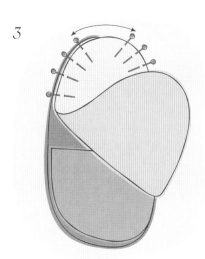

Lay the hot pink sole piece flat on your work surface and place the sequinned upper on top, with the sequins facing down. Place the light pink sole piece on top, sandwiching the upper between the two sole pieces. Pin along the edges and machine stitch to join, leaving a 3-in. (7-cm) opening at the back.

4 Trim the seam allowance to ¼ in. (0.5 cm) and turn the slipper right side out. Trim the edges of the thick wool soles by ½ in. (1.5 cm), and insert them into the slippers. Tuck the fabric edges in at the back opening, pin to hold in place, and hand stitch to finish.

You will need

8 in. (20 cm) hot pink wool mix felt, 39 in. (100 cm) wide

8 in. (20 cm) light pink wool mix felt, 39 in. (100 cm) wide

8 in. (20 cm) thick wool fabric, 39 in. (100 cm) wide

Sequins and paillettes in colors to match fabric

Sewing machine

Needle and matching sewing threads

Fabric pattern pieces required

Hot pink felt: 2 sole pieces, 2 upper pieces

Light pink felt: 2 sole pieces, 2 upper pieces

Thick wool fabric: 2 sole pieces

Take ½-in. (1.5-cm) seam allowances throughout unless otherwise stated.

Techniques

Working with patterns

The patterns on the pull-out sheets included with this book are full size, so you do not need to enlarge them. Different kinds of line indicate different sizes. Before you cut out the paper pattern pieces, highlight the line you need to follow on all pieces with a marker pen.

Making paper patterns

Trace the required pattern pieces onto tissue paper and cut them out. Tissue paper works better than hard tracing paper, as it is soft and easy to pin to the fabric.

Pattern symbols

Patterns are marked with various standard symbols, which show you how to place the pattern on the fabric and also ensure that you can match up different pieces correctly.

Grain line: When you pin the paper pattern to the fabric, any grain line should be placed on the straight grain of the fabric. Make sure that the grain line, which is marked as an arrow, is parallel with the selvage.

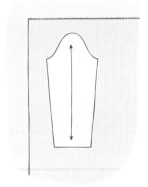

Fold line: This is used for symmetrical pieces—for example, the back panel of a shirt. Fold the fabric in half, right sides together, and place this line of the pattern on the fold.

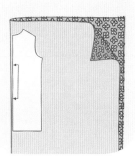

Balance marks: These indicate points that need to be matched across different pattern pieces. Balance marks look like black triangular notches and they need to be transferred from the paper pattern to the fabric. To do this, snip into the fabric wherever there is a notch on the pattern.

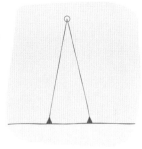

Dart lines: Darts create shaping to ensure a garment fits well. They are marked with triangular lines that indicate the dart seam. To transfer dart lines onto the fabric, snip the notches at the end of each dart line and mark out the dart point by putting a pin through it or by drawing a small dot using tailor's chalk. Take the pattern off and use tailor's chalk to draw lines between the dart point and each notch.

Pocket position: These are circular marks that indicate where the top two corners of the pocket should be positioned. Transfer the marks onto the fabric by putting a pin through them, or by drawing a small dot using tailor's chalk. Make sure you use the relevant mark for your size.

Cutting fabric pieces

1 If your paper patterns are very creased, press them with a cool iron before you pin them to the fabric. Lay the fabric on a large, flat surface and smooth it out.

2 Pin the pattern pieces on top, then carefully cut along the edge of the pattern using sharp fabric scissors. If there are any notches on the edge of the cutting line, remember to snip them before you take the pattern off the fabric. If you have any asymmetrical pattern pieces that you need to cut two of, such as sleeves, make sure you cut a left and a right piece. The easiest way to do this is to cut both pieces at the same time with the fabric folded with right sides together.

3 Transfer any markings such as dart lines or pocket positions to the fabric. You can do this using tailor's chalk, a fabric marker pen, or tailor's tacks.

Interfacing

Interfacing is a synthetic fabric that is used to slightly stiffen and add stability to garment facings and collars. In this book, we have used iron-on interfacings, which have one side coated with a fusible adhesive. Fusible interfacing comes in different weights. To get the right weight, take a scrap of the fabric you are going to use to the store and ask the staff for advice.

1. Re-use the paper pattern to cut the required pieces of interfacing.

2. Lay the interfacing on the wrong side of the fabric piece, adhesive side down. Following the manufacturer's instructions, press firmly with a warm iron for a few seconds to fuse the interfacing to the fabric. Leave to cool.

Basic hand stitches

Some stitches are functional and are used to hold pieces of fabric together, while some are purely decorative.

Basting (tacking) stitch

Basting (tacking) stitch is used to hold pieces of fabric in place until they have been sewn together permanently. The stitches are removed once the permanent stitching is complete. Use a contrasting color of thread, so that you can see it easily.

Knot the thread and, working from right to left, work a long running stitch through all layers.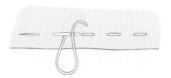

Slipstitch

Slipstitch is an almost invisible method of hemming. It is also used to close openings—for example, in the waist channel of an elasticated waistband.

Working from right to left, slide the needle between the two pieces of fabric, bringing it out on the edge of the top fabric so that the 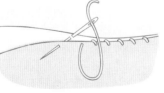 knot in the thread is hidden between the two layers. Pick up one or two threads from the base fabric, then bring the needle up a short distance along, on the edge of the top fabric, and pull through.

Backstitch

Backstitch forms a continuous line of small, evenly spaced stitches. It is useful for outlining motifs.

Work from right to left. Bring the needle up at A, down and B, and up at C. The distance between A and B should be the same as the distance 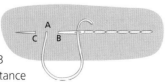 between A and C. To begin the next stitch, insert the needle at A again. Repeat as necessary.

Blanket stitch

This is used as a decorative edging and as a decorative way of appliquéing one piece of fabric to another.

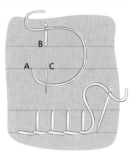

1. Work from left to right. Bring the needle up at A, down at B and up at C, looping the thread under the needle. Pull through.

2. Repeat as necessary.

Satin stitch

Satin stitch is used to fill in open motifs. The stitches should be close together, so that no fabric can be seen between them.

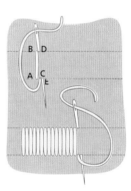

Work from left to right. Bring the needle up at A, down at B, up at C, down and D, and up at E. Repeat as required.

Stab stitch

Stab stitch is a decorative straight stitch that is very easy to work. Simply make even stitches in a straight line, one at a time, holding the needle almost vertically.

Insert the needle at A and take it through to the other side of the fabric. Bring it back up again at B, and repeat as necessary.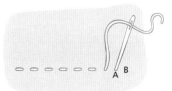

Finishing raw edges

Raw edges need to be finished to prevent them from fraying. Use either of the methods listed below.

Method 1: Zigzag stitch

Use the zigzag stitch on your sewing machine, set to the maximum stitch width and length.

Method 2: Overlocking

Alternatively, for a professional finish, use an overlocking machine, which simultaneously trims and over-edge stitches the seam allowance.

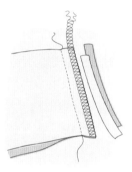

Darts

1 Fold the fabric with right sides together, making sure that the notches at the end of each dart line match up. Pin the fold in place along the dart line.

2 Stitch from the edge of the fabric to the dart point following the chalk line. Do not back tack at the end, and leave enough thread to allow you to tie a knot.

Patch pockets—using a template

1 Trace the pocket pattern onto thin card and cut out.

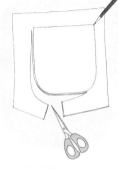

2 Cut away the specified seam allowance to make a template of the pocket.

3 Place the template in the center of the fabric piece, on the wrong side. Wrap the seam allowance over it, steam-pressing flat as you go.

Collars and facings

1 With right sides together, pin and machine stitch the two collar pieces together along the outside edge, leaving the neckline open. Trim the seam allowances and turn the collar right side out. Press the edge.

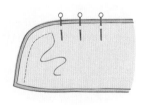

2 Position the collar along the neckline of the shirt, making sure that any balance marks match up. Pin and stitch in place.

3 Join the front facings to the back neck facing by stitching along the shoulder seams. Press the seam allowances open and zigzag stitch or overlock the inside edge of the facing.

4 With right sides together, place the facing on the shirt, sandwiching the collar between the shirt and the facing. Pin the facing in place and stitch from the hem, up around the neckline, and back down to the hem on the other side. Trim the seam allowances, turn the facing to the inside of the shirt, and press the front edge.

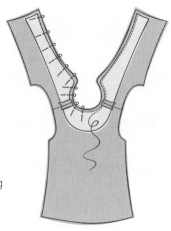

5 On the inside of the shirt, pin the back neck facing to the back shirt piece along the facing edge. Stitch along the facing edge from shoulder to shoulder.

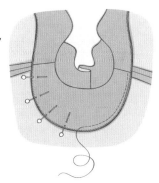

Sleeves

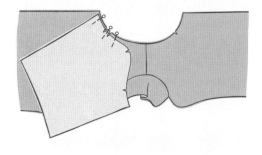

1 Turn the shirt inside out. Matching the balance marks on the garment and sleeve, pin the sleeve to the armhole, right sides together. Pin the underarm seam.

2 Baste (tack) the sleeve in place and clip the seam allowance. Stitch the seam, overlock or zigzag stitch the raw edges together, and press toward the sleeve.

3 Match up the underarm and side seam edges and pin in place. Stitch from cuff to hem, overlock or zigzag stitch the edges together, and press the seam allowances toward the front.

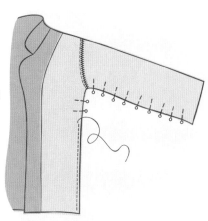

Assembling pants and shorts

1 Overlock or zigzag stitch the raw edges at the leg and crotch, leaving the top edge and hems unfinished.

2 Pin, then machine stitch the front legs to the back legs along the inside leg seams.

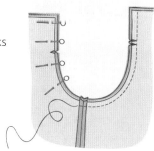

3 With right sides together, matching the balance marks and inside leg seams, pin, baste (tack), and machine stitch the crotch, stopping 1½ in. (4 cm) from the top edge at the center back.

4 With right sides together, stitch the front legs to the back legs at the side seams. Press all seam allowances open as you go.

Marking button holes

The number of buttonholes and the distance between them will vary depending on the style and size you are making. The position of the top button is indicated on the pattern by means of a circular mark. Measure the distance from the top button position down to the hem. Divide this measurement by the number of buttons you are going to have. This will give you the distance between each button. Mark the position for each buttonhole out along the center front of the garment.

Making buttonholes

Different sewing machines use slightly different methods for stitching buttonholes, so follow the instruction in your sewing machine manual. Most machines have a special buttonhole foot; some even have a completely automated buttonhole function.

1 Mark the size of the buttonhole on the fabric, using tailor's chalk or a fabric marker pen.

2 Machine stitch a tight line of zigzag stitches along each side of the marked line, with a block of stitches at either end.

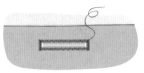

3 Put a pin across the buttonhole at one end. Starting at the other end, cut a slit between the lines of zigzag stitches using small, sharp scissors or an unpicker/seam ripper.

Cutting a bias strip

1 Fold the fabric over so that the cut edge is parallel with the selvage. Lightly press the folded edge to give a crease mark. Open the fabric out again.

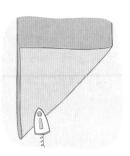

2 The crease indicates the bias grain line, which runs diagonally across the fabric. Using a ruler or set square and tailor's chalk, mark out the length and width of the required bias strips, aligning them with the crease mark. Cut along the chalk lines.

3 To join bias strips place two lengths at right angles to each other, right sides together, and stitch. Press the seam allowances open.

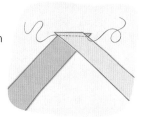

Making a rouleau tube

There is a useful tool for making rouleax called a rouleau hook. If you have one of these, follow the instructions from the manufacturer. Otherwise, use the following method.

1 On your sewing machine, pull out the top and bottom threads until you have about 18 in. (45 cm) free. Fold your bias strip in half, placing the long threads inside the fold. Stitch down the center of the folded strip, making sure you do not stitch over the threads inside.

2 Trim the seam allowances as close as possible to the stitching line. Pull the threads through the loop to turn the rouleau right side out.

Adding piping to an edge

1 Place the piping cord in the center of the bias strip and fold the edges over, trapping the cord inside.

2 With right sides together, aligning the raw edges, sandwich the bias strip in between the pieces to be edged and pin in place. Stitch, using a half-presser foot to get the stitching very close to the piping cord.

Gathering by machine

1 Set the stitch length to the longest setting. Machine stitch two parallel lines ¾ in. (2 cm) apart along the edge to be gathered.

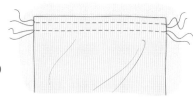

2 Secure all the threads at one end with a pin and gently pull the two top threads at the other end to gather the fabric to the required length, making sure the gathers are even. Secure these threads with another pin.

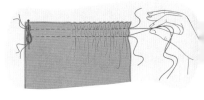

Templates

To use these templates, enlarge them to the required size on a photocopier and, using a thick black pencil, trace onto tracing paper. Turn the tracing paper over, place it on card, and scribble over the pencil lines to transfer the design. Iron fusible bonding web to the wrong side of your appliqué fabric. Cut out the card shape, place it on the paper-backed side of the fabric, and draw around it with a pencil. Cut out the motif, peel away the backing, and iron the motif in place on the garment.

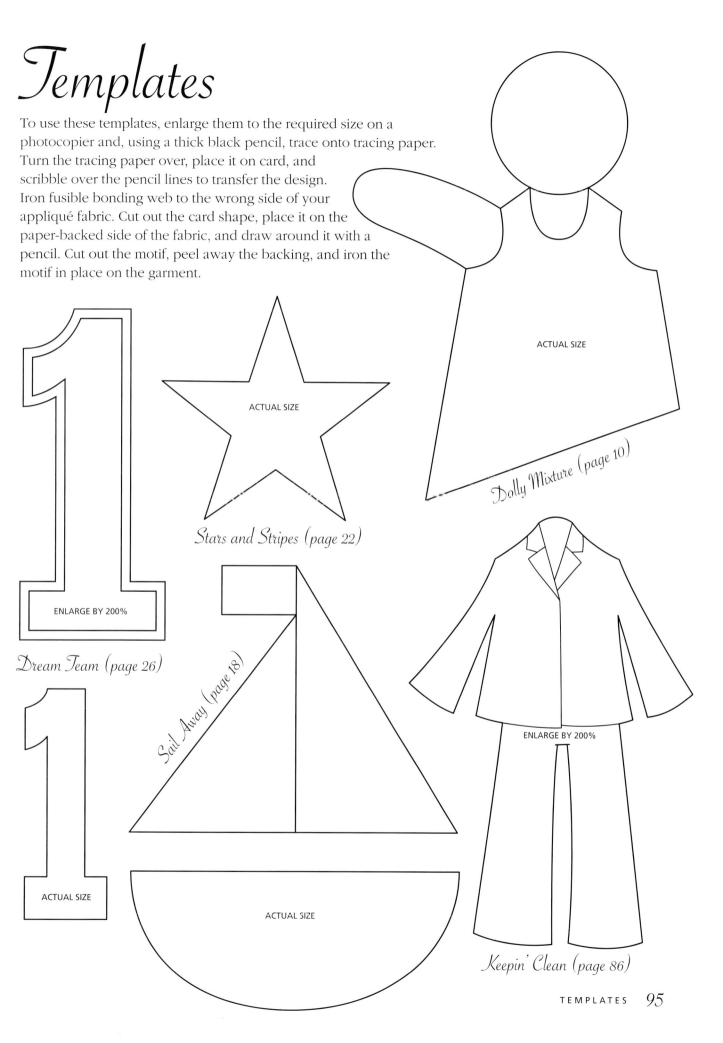

ACTUAL SIZE

Dolly Mixture (page 10)

ACTUAL SIZE

Stars and Stripes (page 22)

ENLARGE BY 200%

Dream Team (page 26)

Sail Away (page 18)

ACTUAL SIZE

ACTUAL SIZE

ENLARGE BY 200%

Keepin' Clean (page 86)

Index